(✳✳✳) aube/crépuscule
matin froid, lumière nordique

lumière blanc chaud jaune vert
rose pétale blanc
légères striures/pluie grise

pluie bleue froid

bleu ciel grisé

striures diffusion haute blanche
blanc halo lumière froide jaune
indigo clair/bleu violet
bleu indigo violacé

ciel or ambrer dans l'ambre
violet pourpre magenta clair en lumière rasante

violet bleu

bleu outremer violacé
bleu phtalo intense
bleu cyan moyen intense

172,5 × 136,5 cm

encre s/ papier Fab.

format ≈ carré

ciel cyan clair rose / lisière jaune aude /
fleur carmin liquide ombre / sol bleu phtalo

diffusa brumeuse

ciel cyan liquide clair de ciel

rose parme bleuté d'éclaircie

liquidité solaire
jaune aude tirant au vert lumière

couleur diffuse brune rouge

tiédie d'horizon brun vert aveuglé

fleur carmin liquide d'ombre

moiré d'aurore boréale
terre d'ombre violacé
violet pourpre
violet bleu froid
bleu indigo soutenu
bleu phtalo lumière
bleu phtalo turquoise

144 × 135 cm

encre s/ papier

# CLAIRE CHESNIER

To Lou-Gabriel

© JBE Books, 2024
Artwork cover:
240523, 162 × 136 cm, 2023
Courtesy THE PILL® Gallery
Photo © Fabrice Seixas



ISBN 978-2-36568-104-9

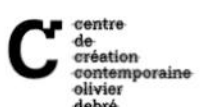 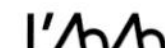 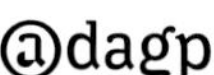

# CLAIRE CHESNIER

JBE BOOKS

*A possible definition of Claire Chesnier's work in progress*

    1. Make a vessel.
    2. Fill it with liquid (preferably water).
    3. Make a pipette or dropper.
    4. Use the pipette or dropper to pick up a small amount of ink.
    5. Drop a drop of ink into the vessel.
    6. Take the container and place it in daylight.
    7. Observe.

This is not the work of an alchemist, but of a mason or a monk.
The rest lies with her...

*Jean-Michel Alberola*

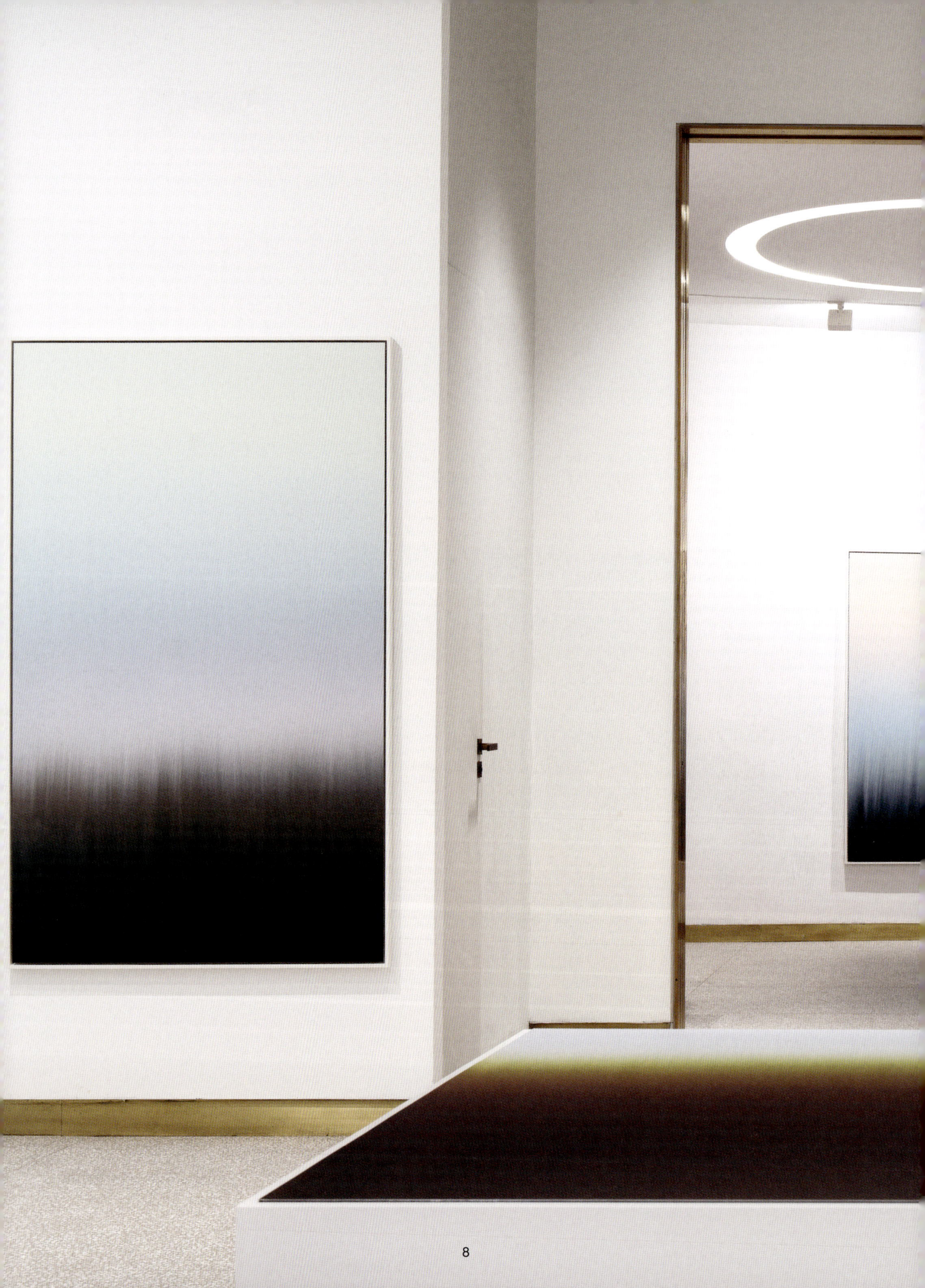

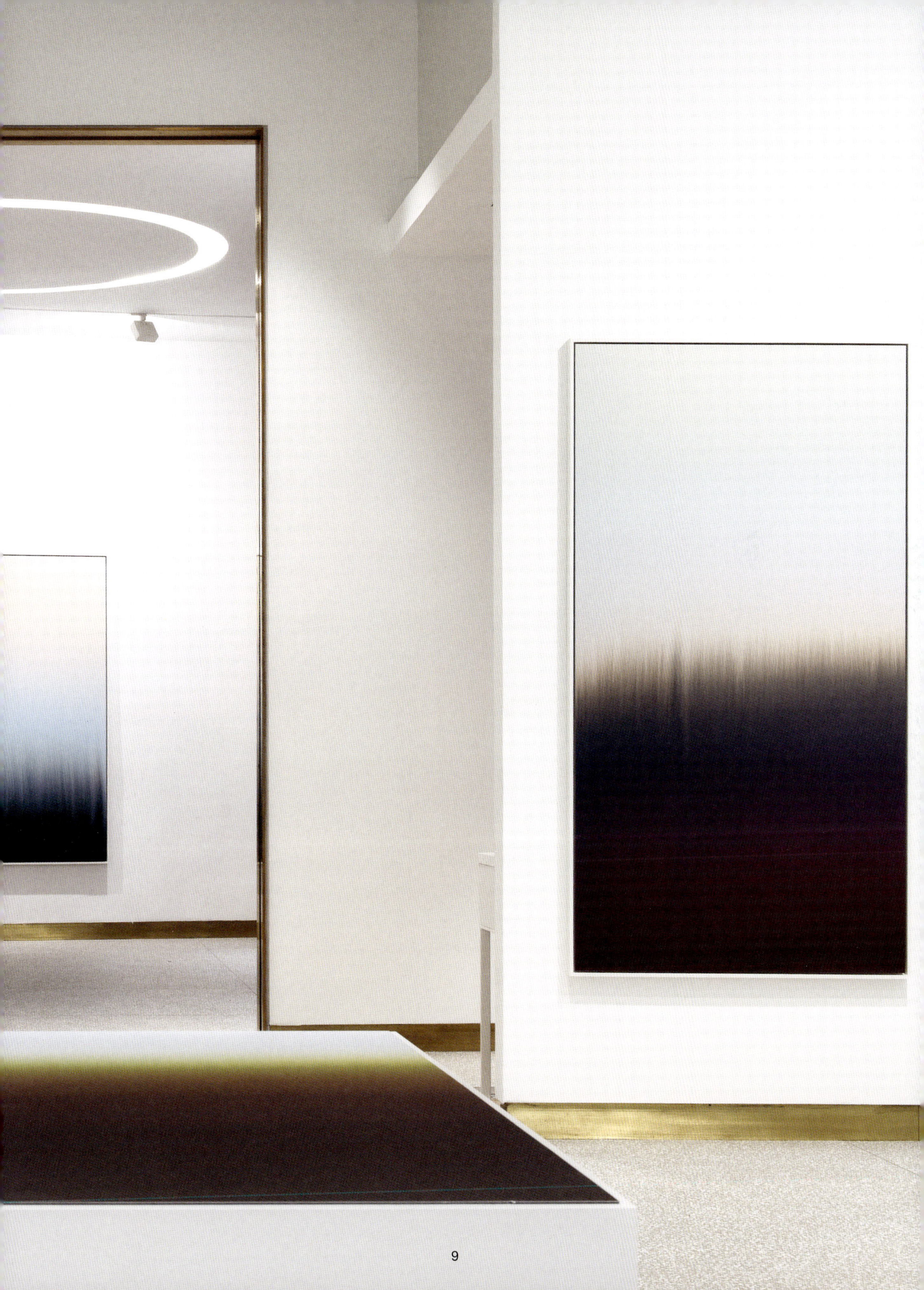

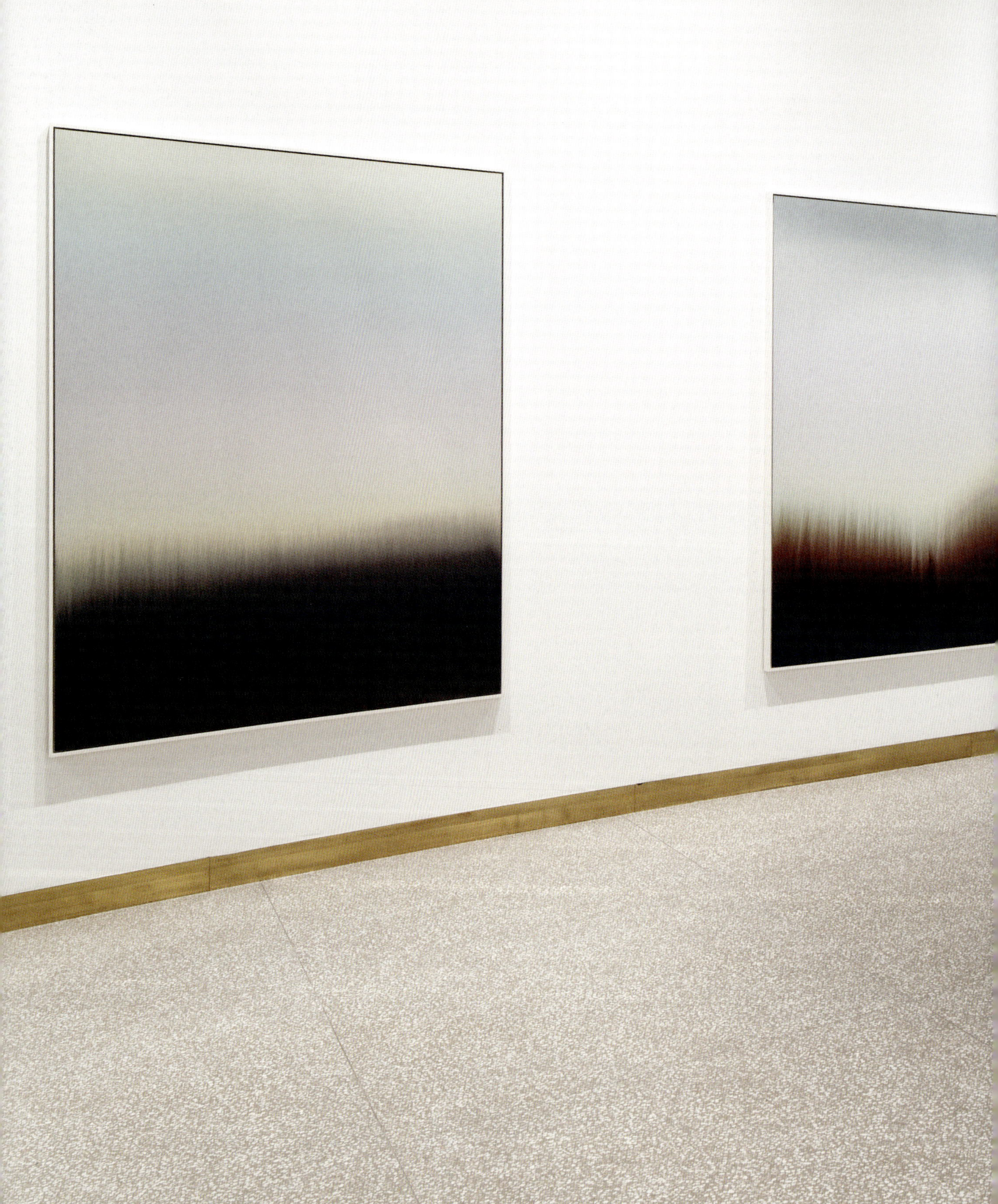

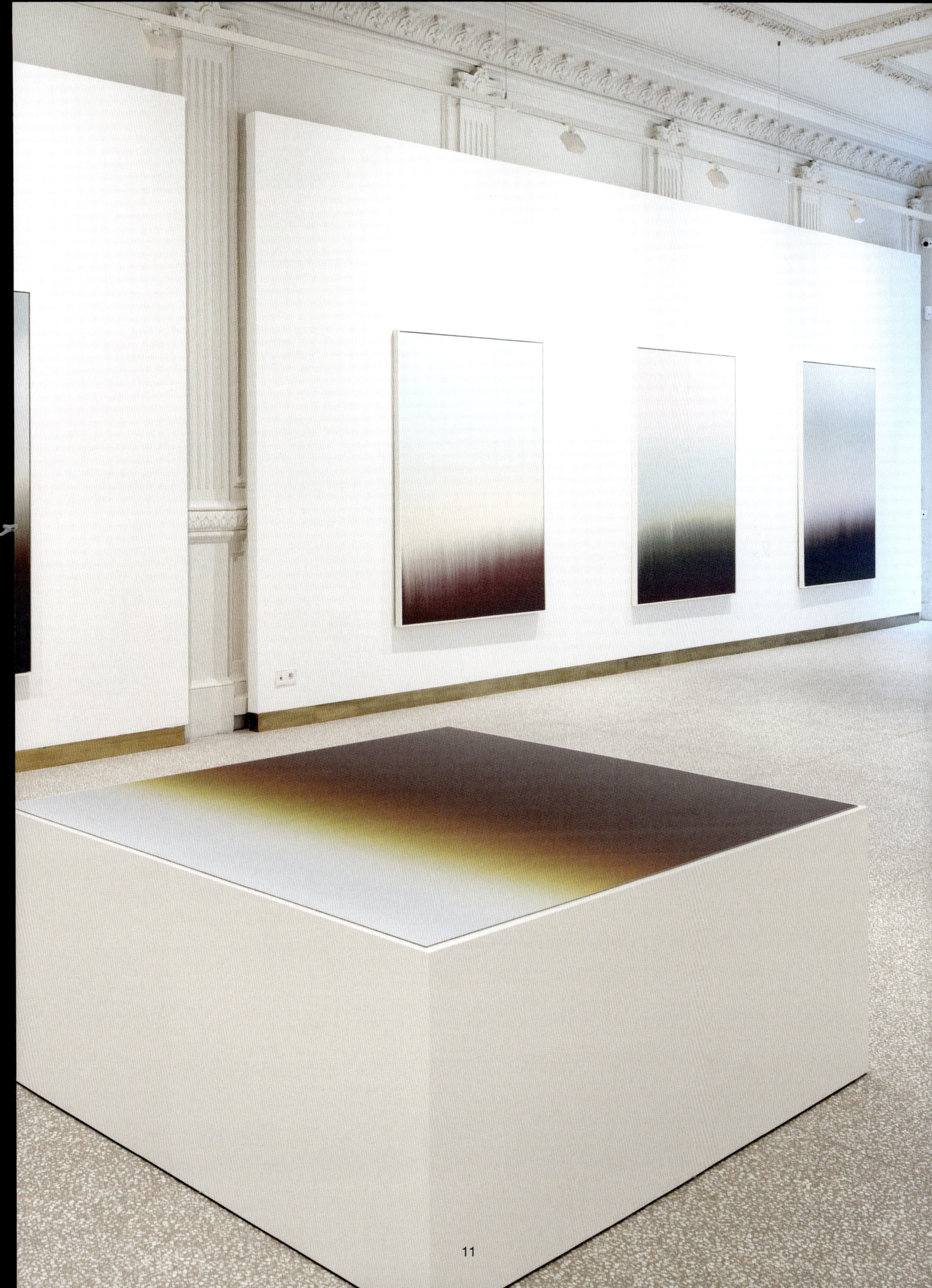

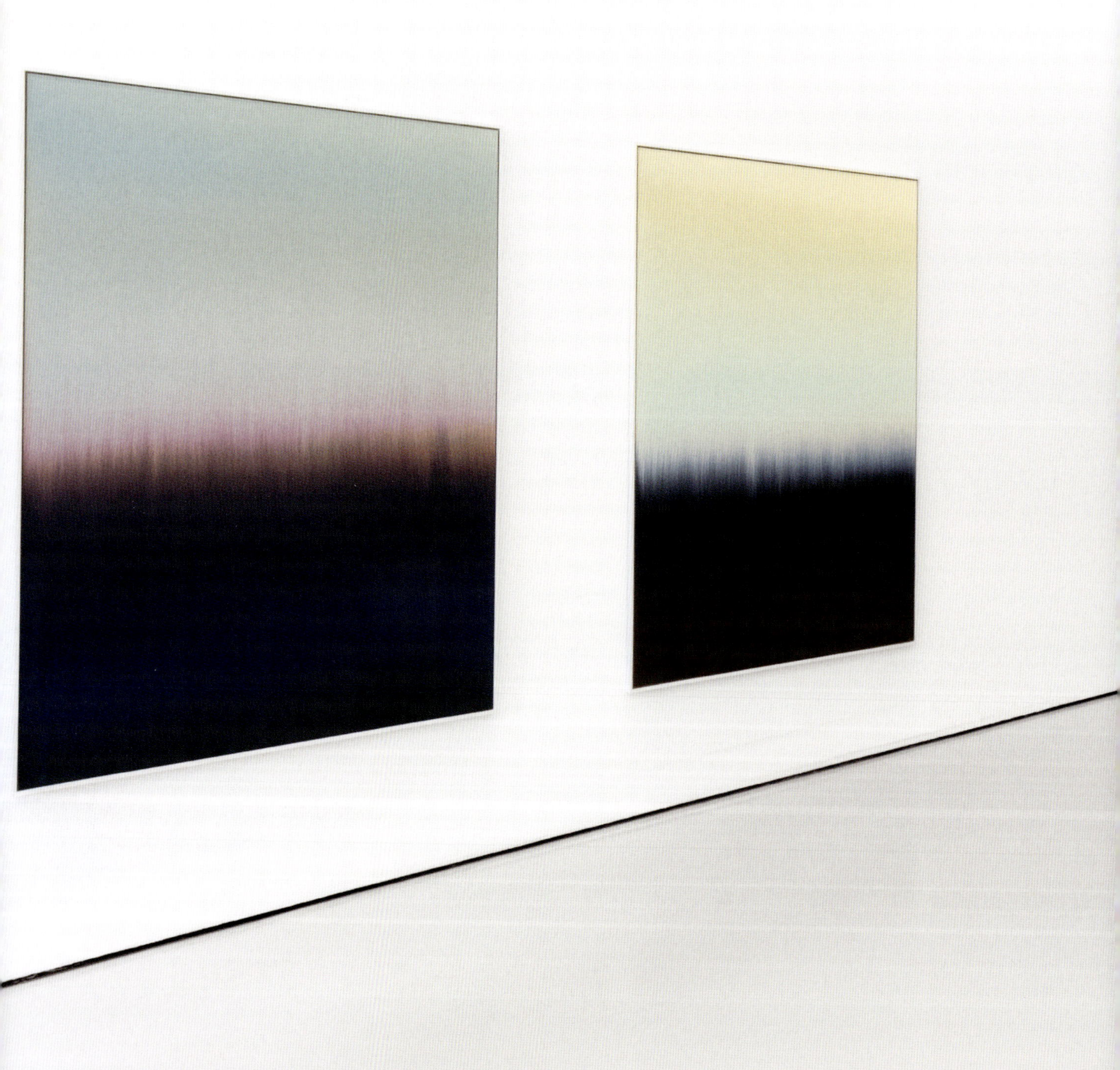

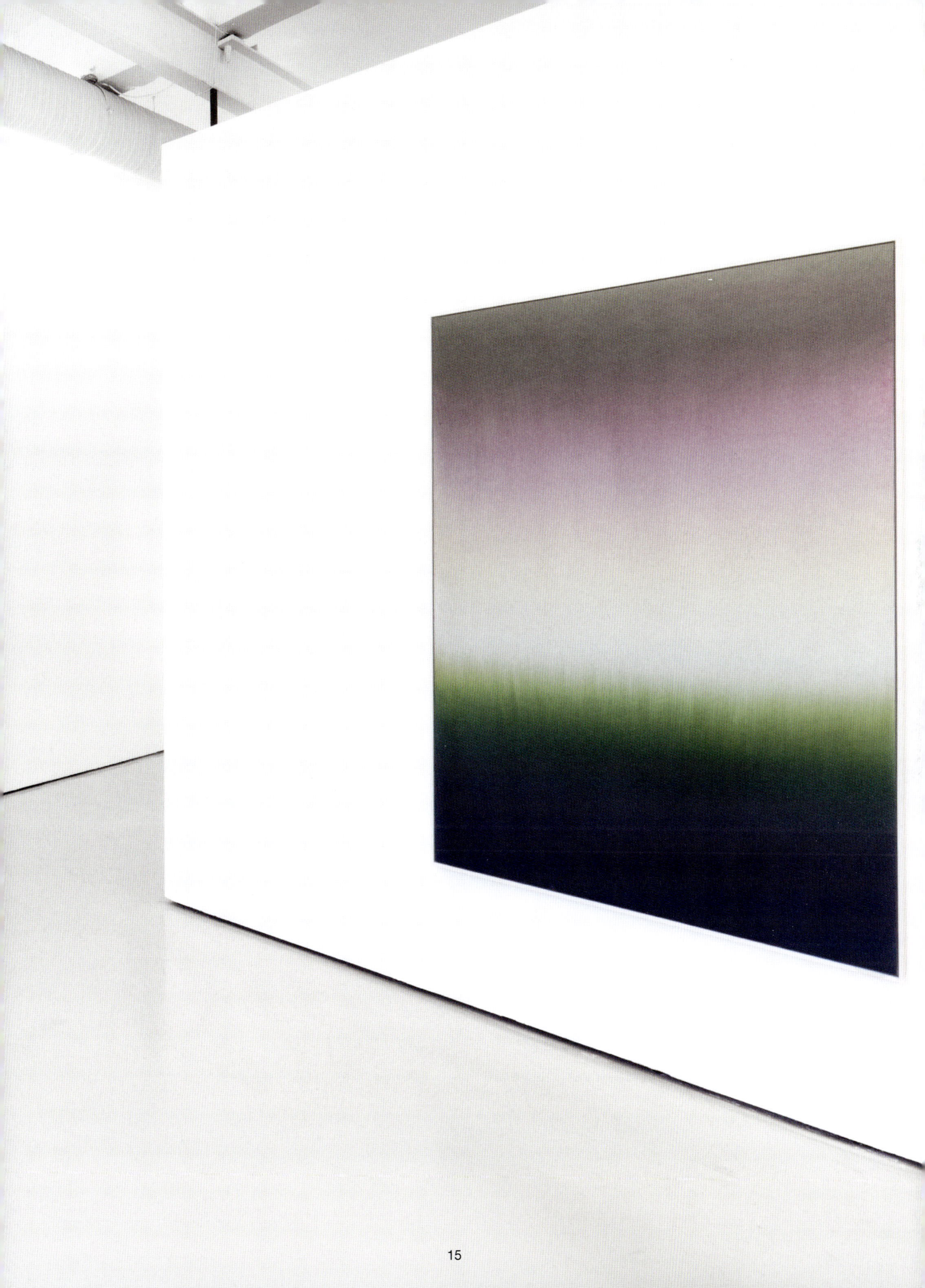

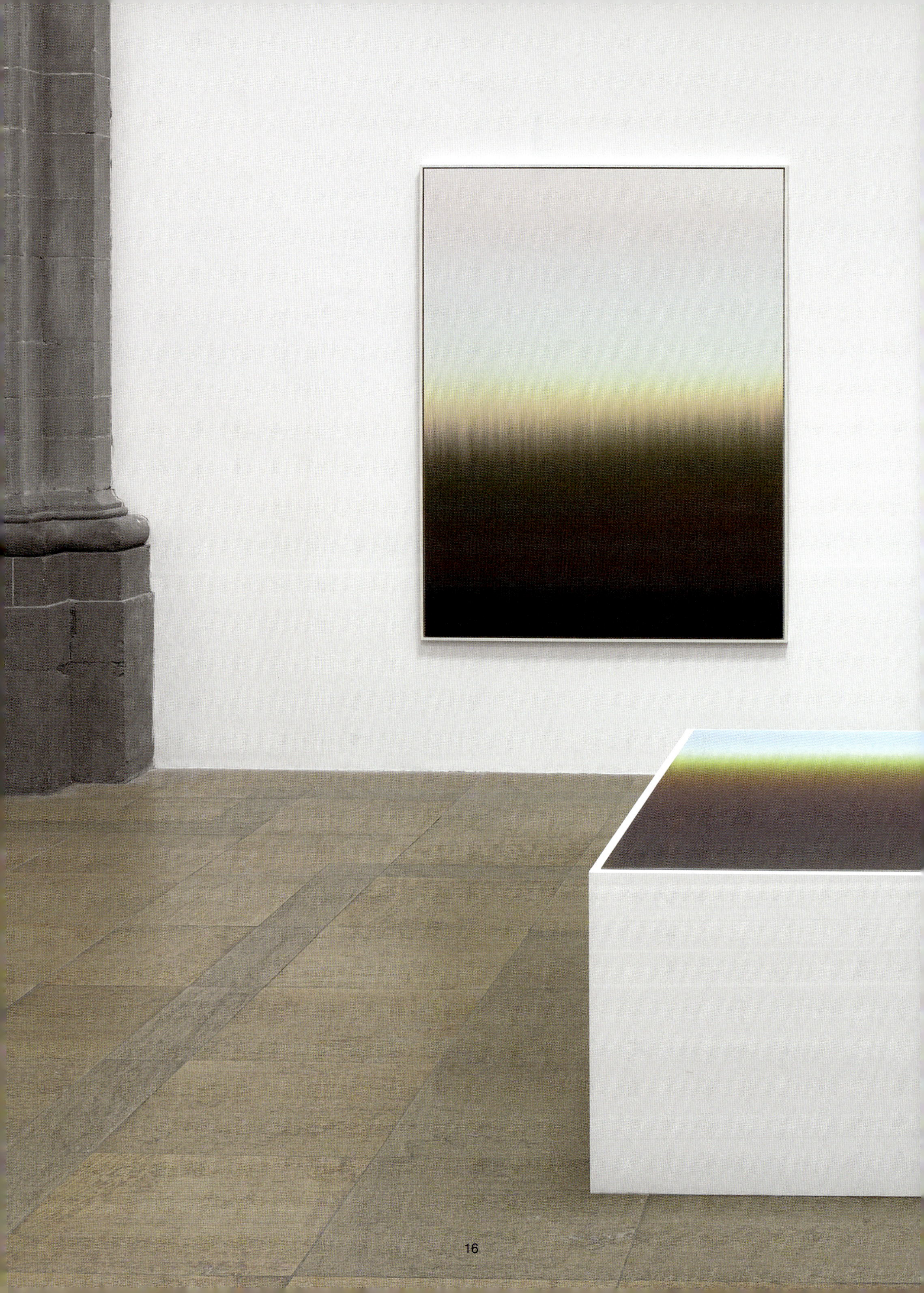

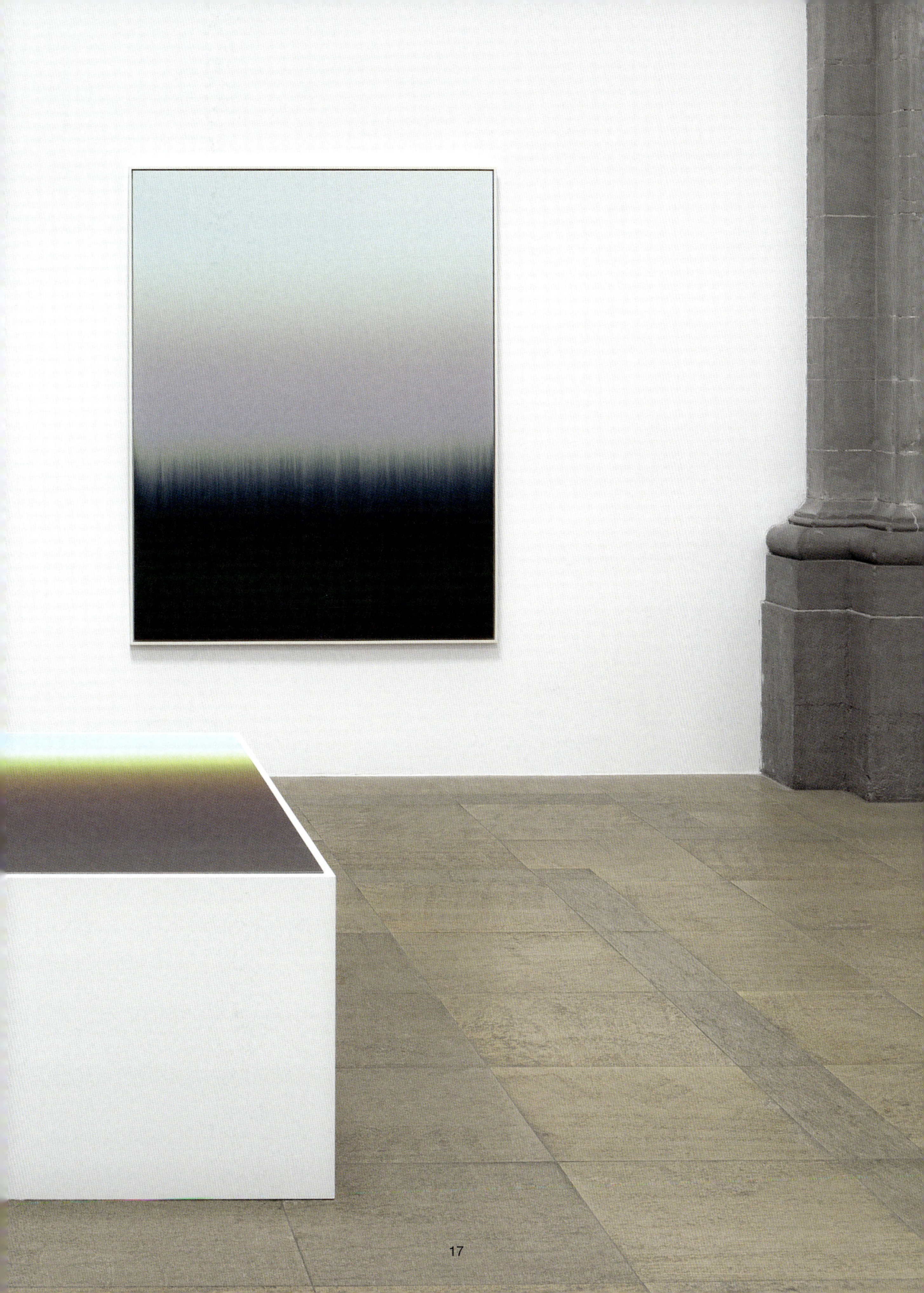

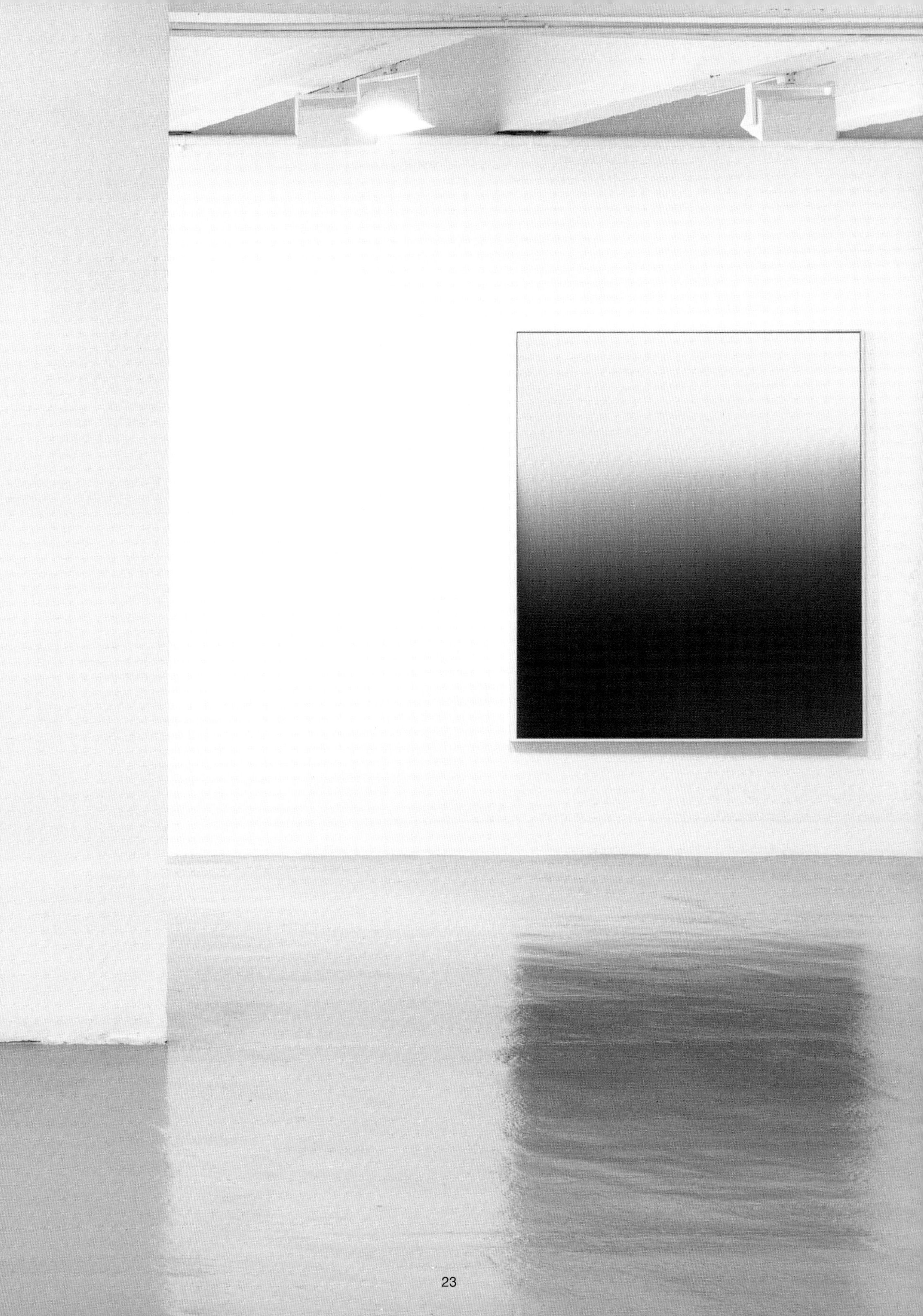

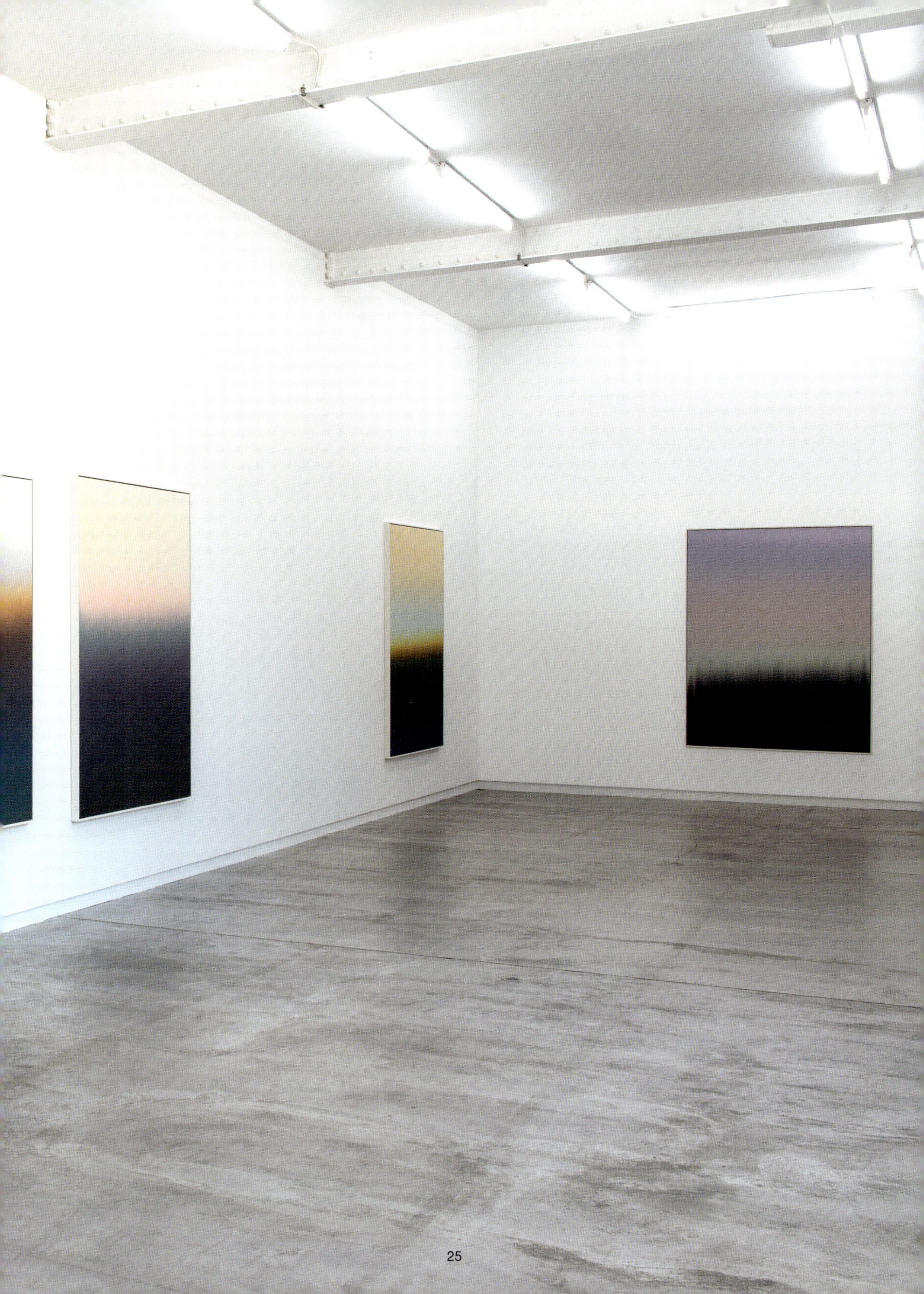

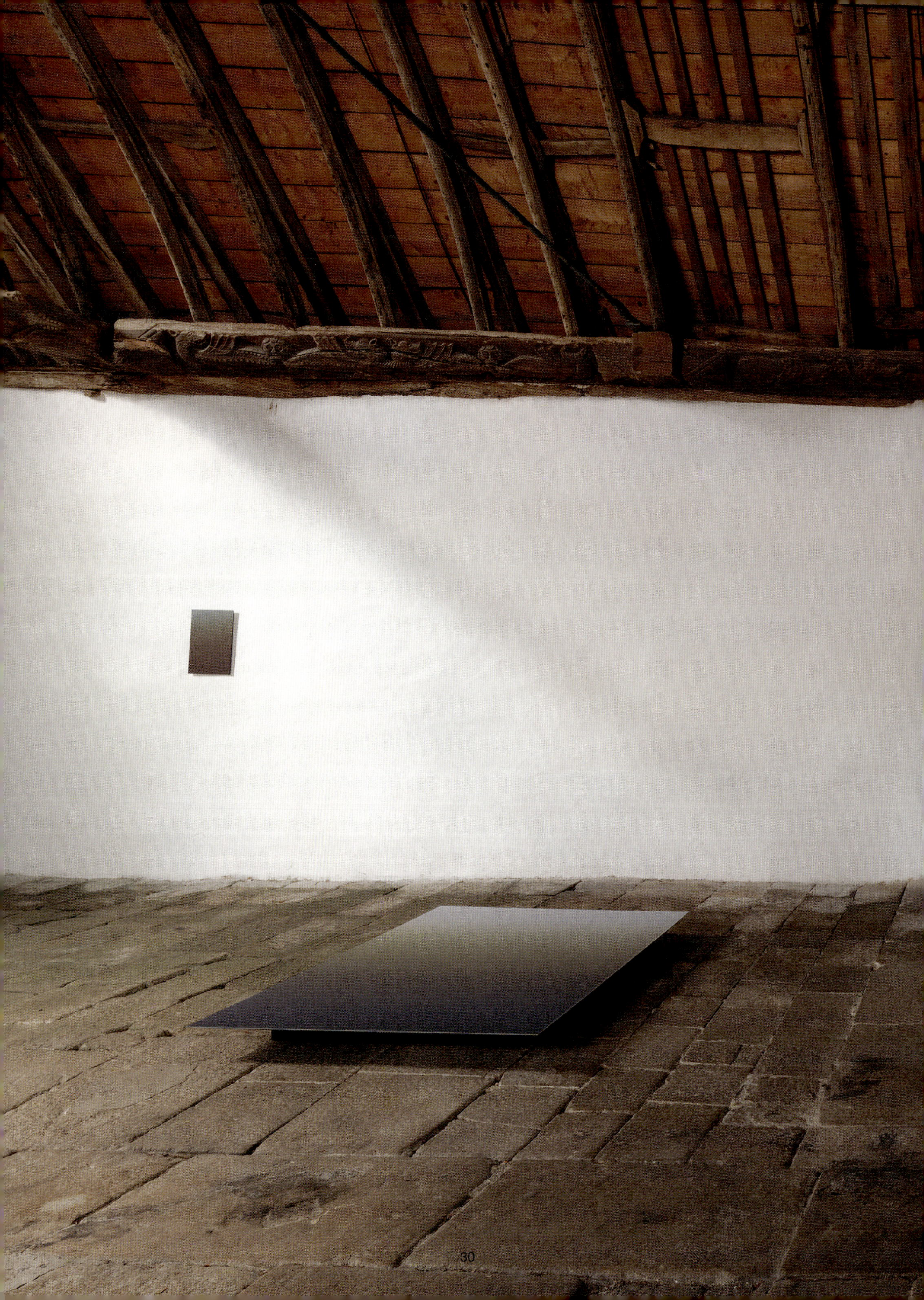

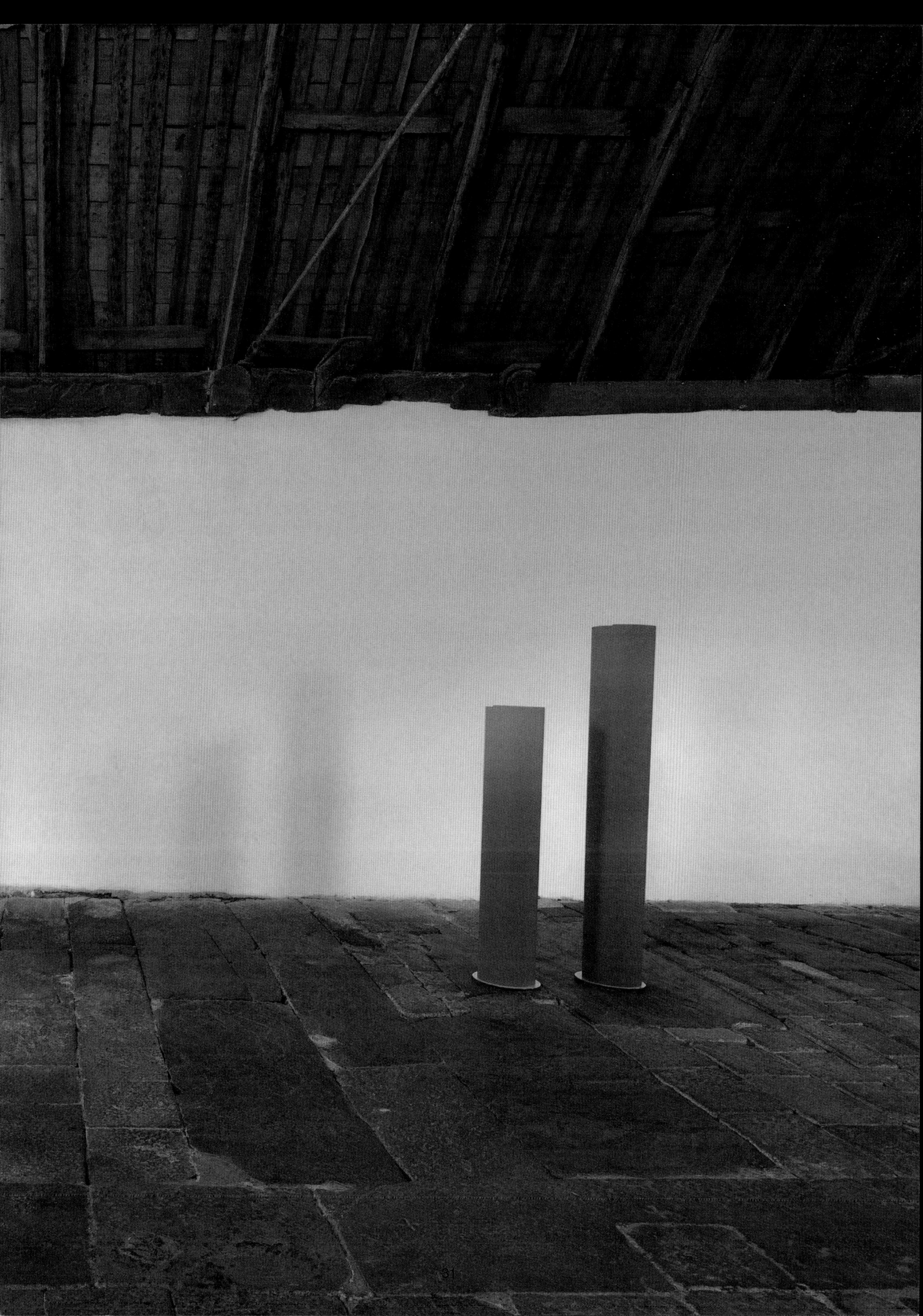

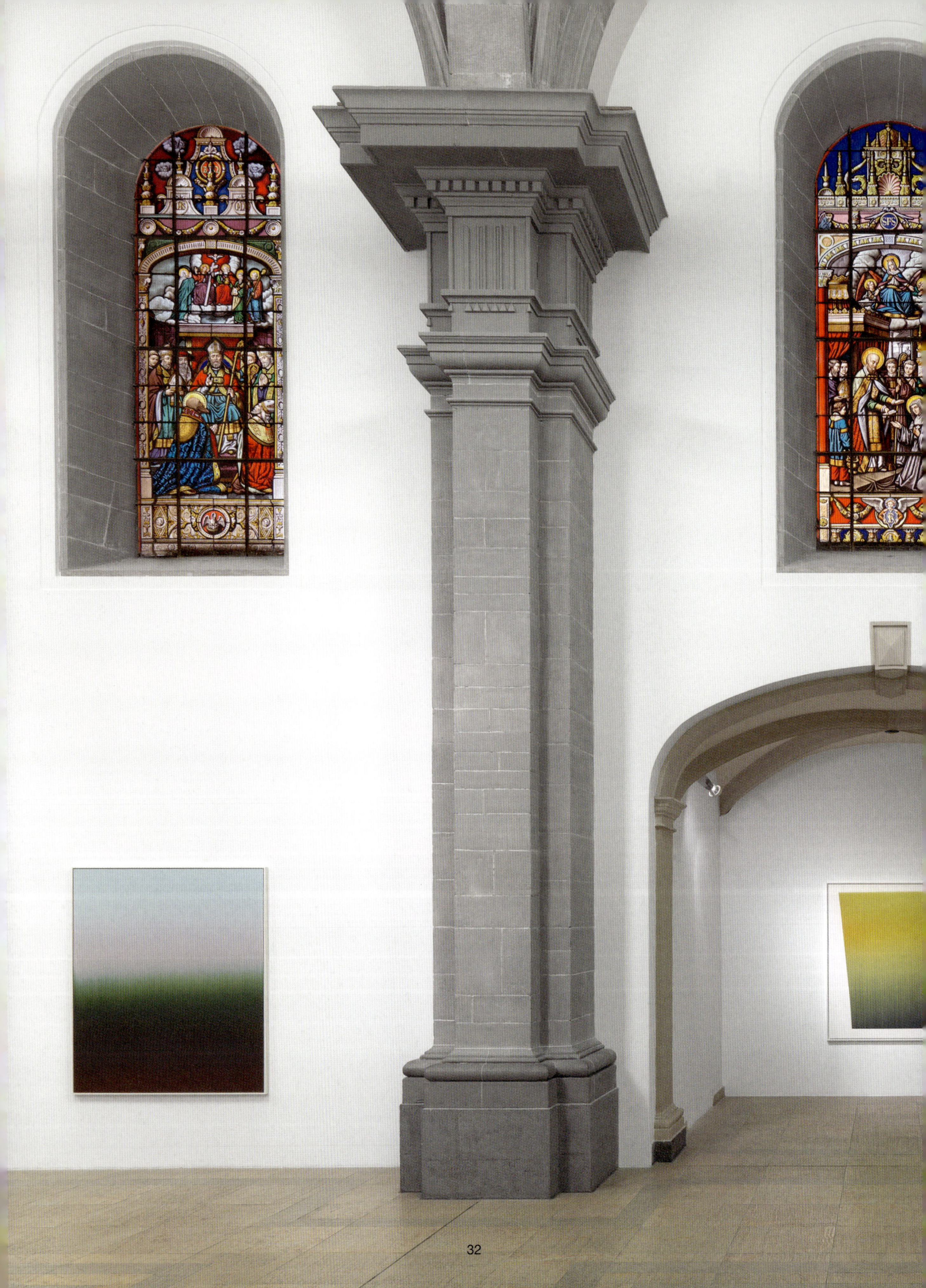

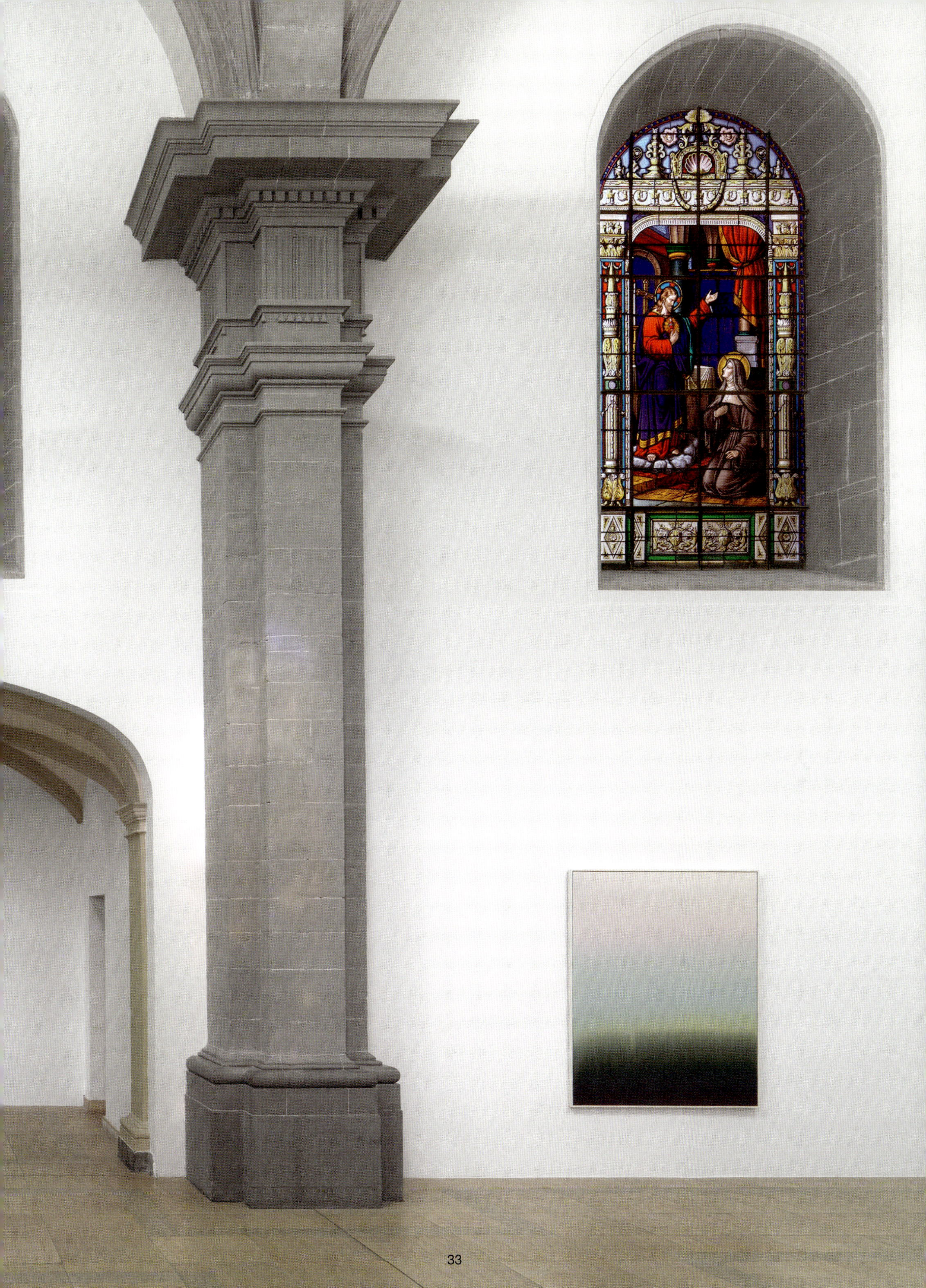

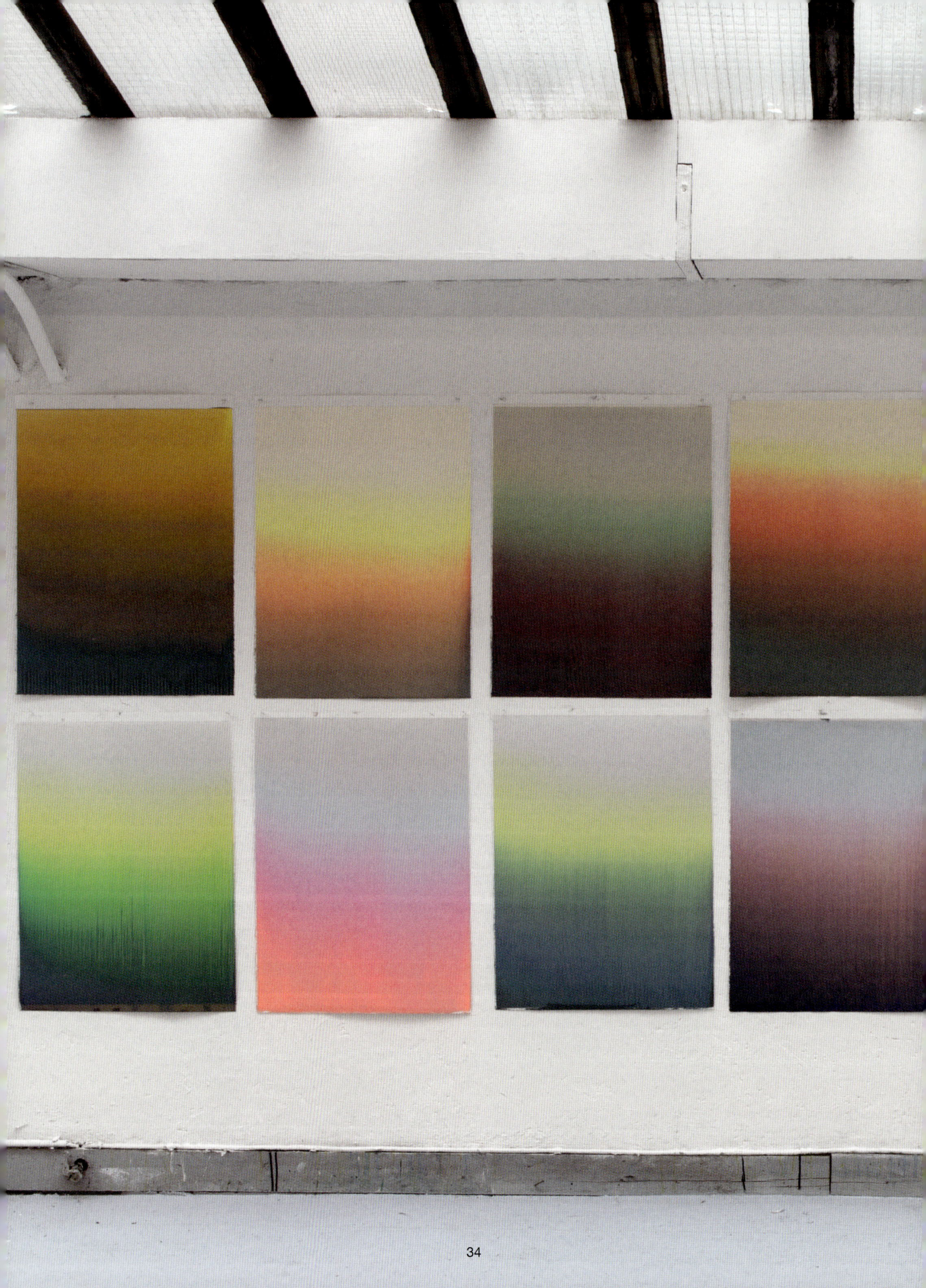

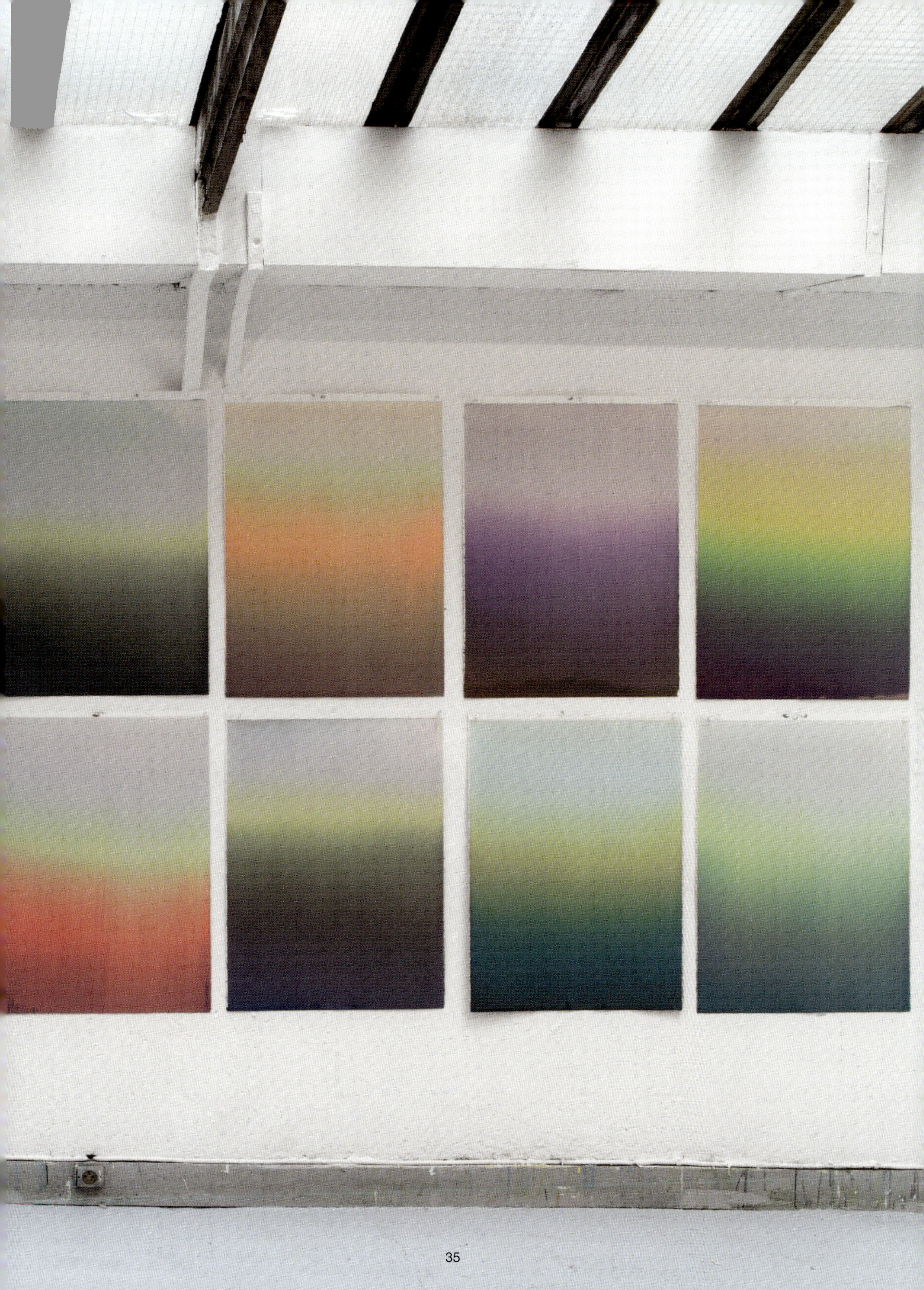

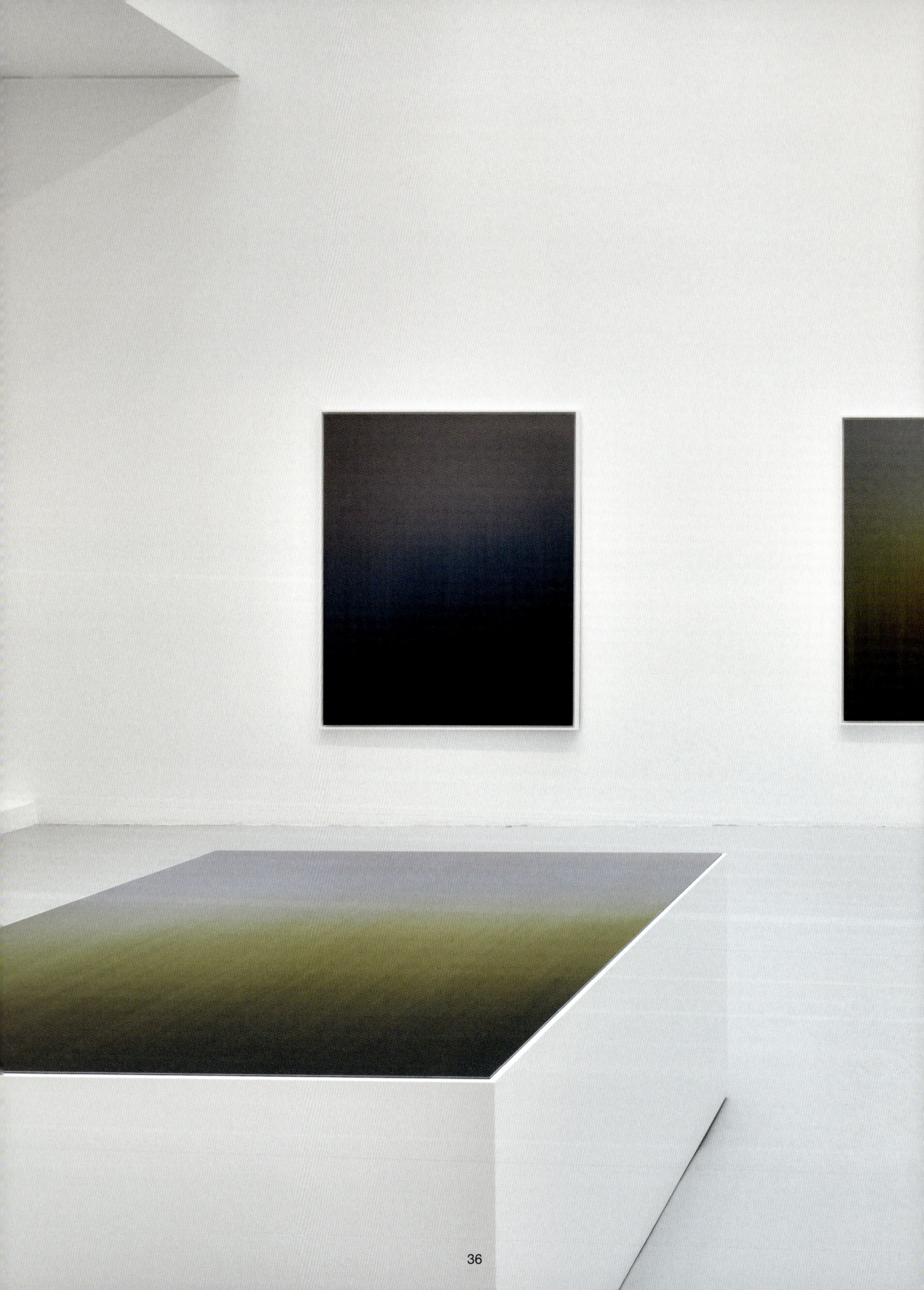

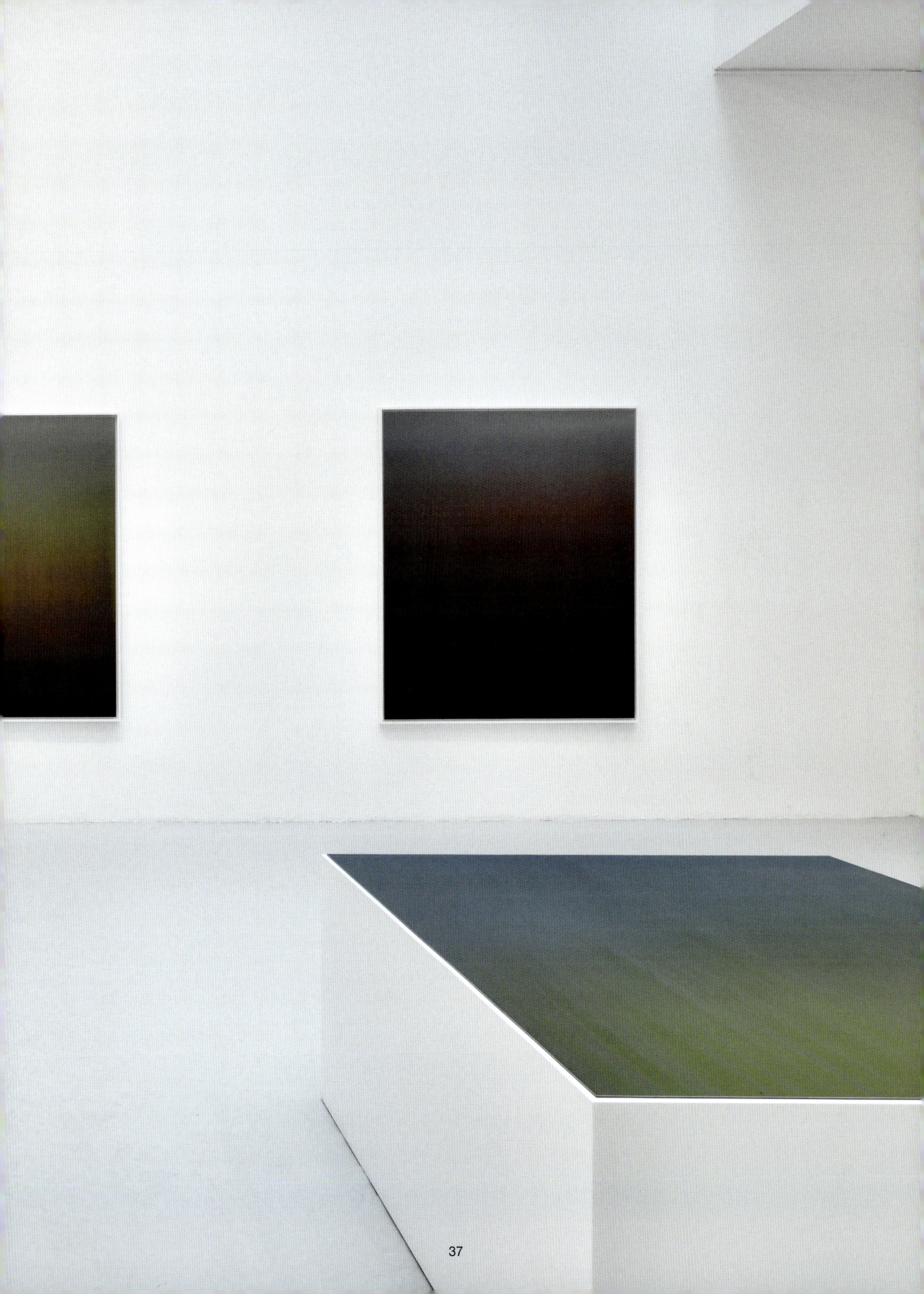

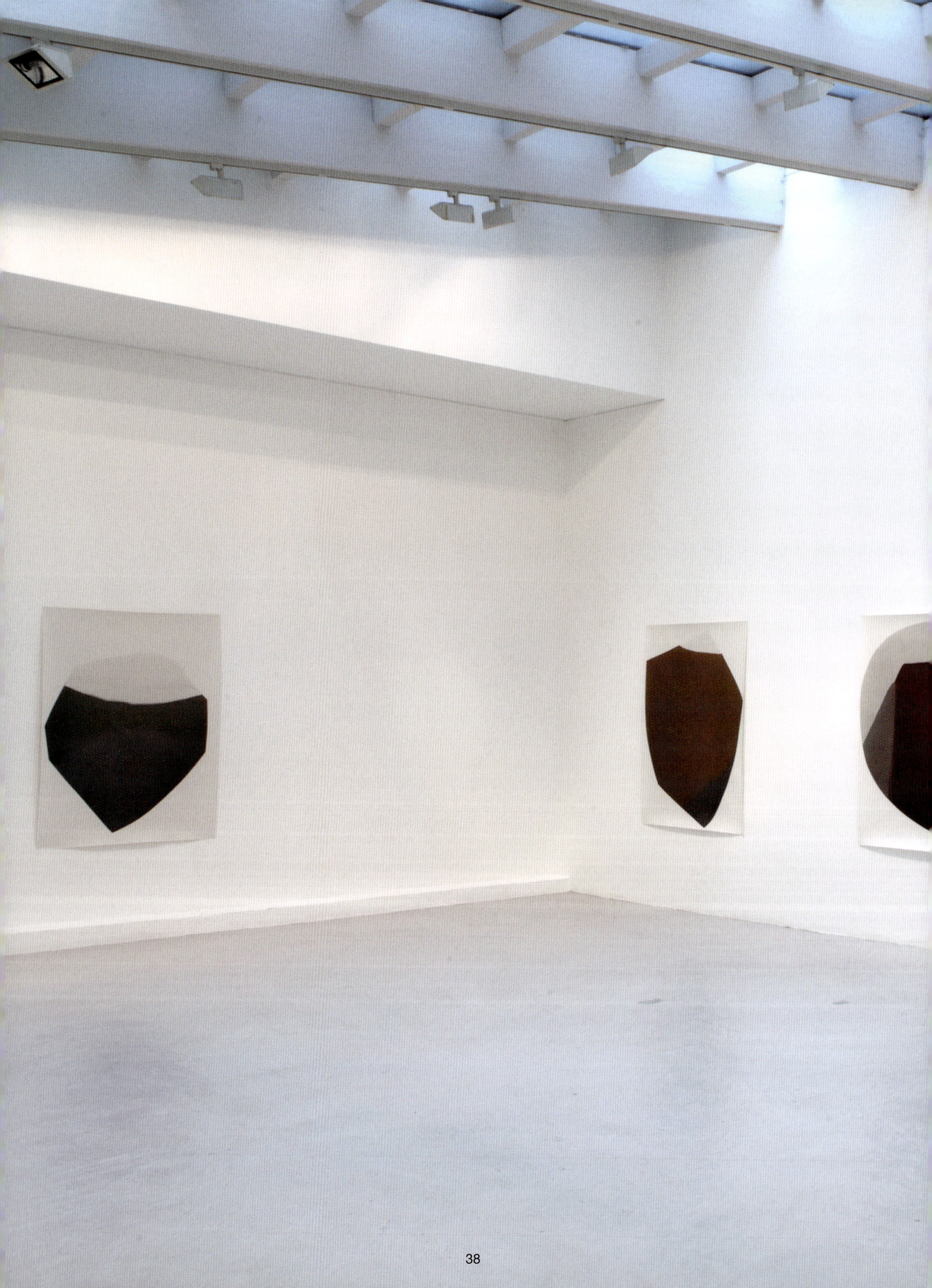

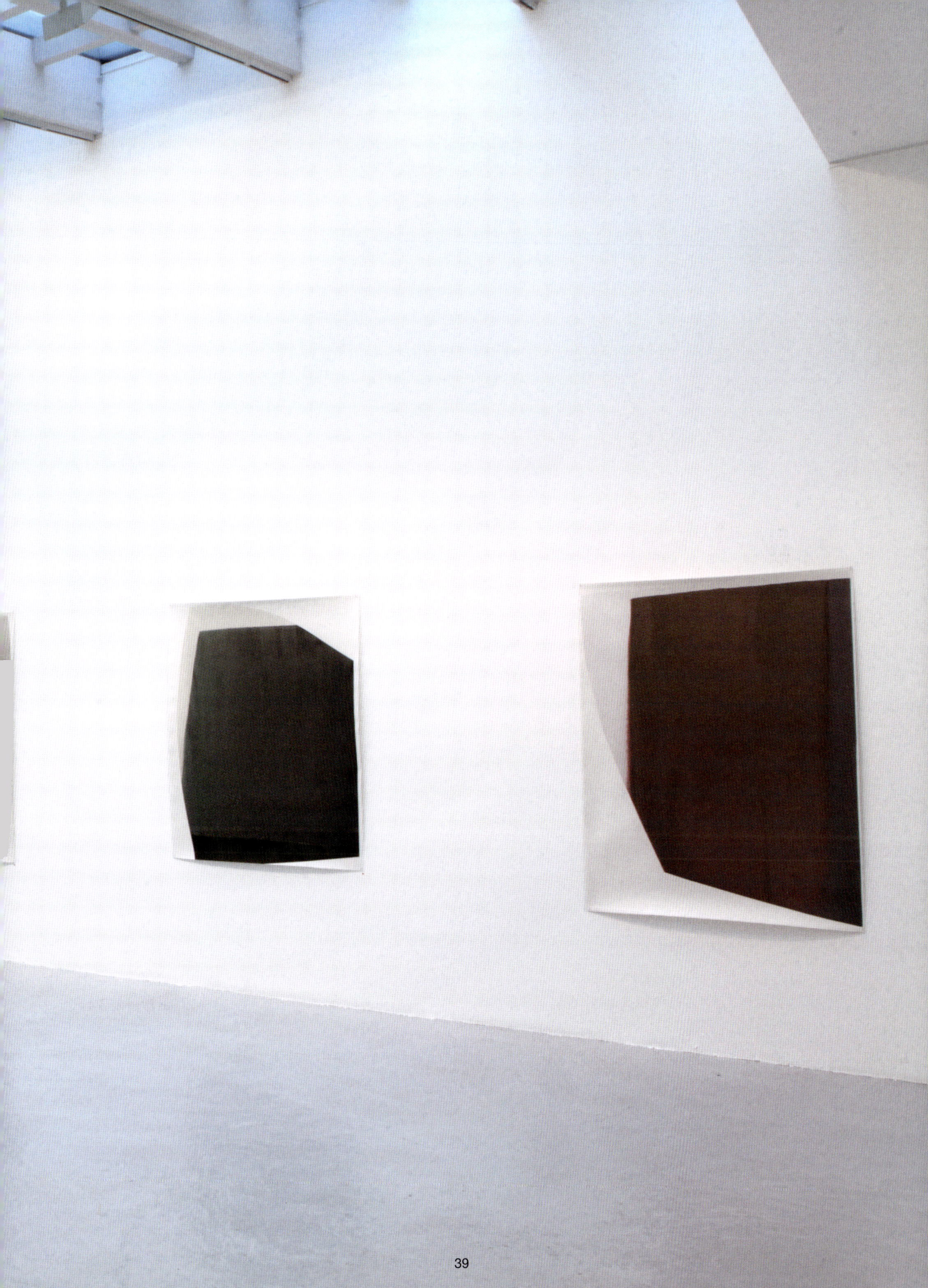

1. *Décamérez! Des nouvelles de Boccace* by Nathalie Koble (Macula, Spring 2021).

Sometimes painting appears in literature. You open a book and there it is. Transferred to a picture on the page. You do not know much about it, you are not aware of its size, its material, its light, you do not understand it, but the image presents itself and sometimes lingers on your retina for a long time.

I first came across one of Claire Chesnier's paintings in a book celebrating a shared experience of reading and writing inspired by Boccaccio's *Decameron*, a book that emerged from the confines of lockdown, seeking breakthroughs, openings, explorations of the interactions between language, fiction and life.[1] The image was printed full-page with large white margins so that it could breathe, inscribe its own surface, in the fading tones of an epiphany, a rose, a dewdrop, a sunset, from earth to mother-of-pearl. There it was a simple bookmark, a punctuation mark, a trace left by reading, a feeling. A few weeks later, it would no longer be just a picture in a book, and I would find myself in front of it.

The studio appears at the bend of a canal-like corridor that one climbs up and at the end of which the space opens and widens. Claire Chesnier precedes me, as does the smell of ink and solvents in the air. The wooden floor creaks. It takes me a few seconds to steady myself on the threshold, dizzy. A lot of sky. It's a spring day.

Large sheets of paper are nailed to the walls, floating lightly, all in a format known as "*à la française*" or "portrait"—a support longer than it is wide. There are five of them. Large sheets of paper on the walls, large sheets that slowly animate the room: they rise and fall, evaporate and settle, breathe in and out. A vertical breath that tells me that painting here is above all a sensation, that the eyes are not the only mode of encounter, not everything in front of the painting, that it is my body that looks.

Here is a place of light and calm that erases the pressure of the metropolis, a unique place, high up, suspended between Earth and sky, an in-between place. I scan the walls first where the sheets of paper, like large windows, blend the near and the far, the solid and the airy, giving the room an almost palpable depth and thickness. Their dimensions are almost identical without being exactly the same, a strange discrepancy visible to the naked eye that allows me to grasp them as a whole, a kind of series that repeatedly executes the same gesture.

This gesture is the *gesture of color*. A gesture that forces you to surrender to color, to fall under its spell and, in this state of surrender, to bring space and time to life, to bring painting to life. I write *color* but

I am no longer so sure of what I see, of the nature of this substance that at first glance borders on the miraculous: at once light and matter, surface and volume, experience and feeling. What I do perceive, however, is that it is complete and unhindered, connected, I don't know how, to a twin hand, with this airy, silent movement that seems to float on the paper. And so *simple*, so autonomous, carried by no drawing and no form, no motif and no meaning, that it seems to have become painting itself, painting that is about nothing other than itself, just painting. The strange feeling that my body is gradually consolidating its contours, that my movements—walking, stopping, sitting, standing, approaching—my gestures, my voice, my breathing are breaking away, clear, as if my presence is sinking into the atmosphere of the room, its corpuscular grain, its silence.

The room is saturated with vibrations, crackling with a thousand little tremors, and we do not speak. I feel rhythms—largos, accelerations, beats. There is no doubt that together we are experiencing the difficulty of putting painting into words, of reducing it to a statement, even more, of discussing it, words at this point of our encounter still far away, imprecise, and like obstacles.

The large sheet of watercolor paper is soaked in water, then covered with several layers of ink, always very diluted, with a brush. The artist's hand flows in the billowing pigments, accompanying them, subjecting them to gravity—the painter works on a vertical surface—and finally withdraws from the paint to let it happen, to let it express itself, completely alive, and it is this gesture that, like a ritual, circumscribes her work as a painter. She writes, "*I change my movements according to the ups and downs of the light, sometimes sudden, dominating my movement, sometimes cautious and reserved, waiting for me to intervene and face this great flow without removing it from the brush bed.*" She adds, "*Without drifting away from the subject of the painting, drifting into the painting and redirecting it, supported by the fluidity that overwhelms the gesture and the intention.*" A practice that serenely, radically uses the surface, bringing glaze, veiling through transparency. Work that relies on the organic materiality of the pigments and their evolution over time: not a process, she writes, but "*what happens for me.*"

I gradually fall into an immersive time, dissident, detached from the pace of the outside world. Time is almost palpable here, the spans of time intertwine, engulf the space, stagnate, flow. It is the time of our bodies, which will soon be synchronized with that of the pigments layered on the surfaces, attuned to this movement that goes from one end of the paper to the other, creating each time a moving threshold, which I first perceive as waiting, as tension, implying an inevitable *progression*.

No matter how much I move to the side, away from these images and back again, I cannot decide whether they are monochromatic variations of a single pigment or polychromatic hues that dilute, generate and scatter several others, and this undecidable problem offers a kind of revelation: there is no more hue, no more tint, the definition of chromatic tonality is transcended, there is only *color*, color that passes before me and meets me, that passes over the large sheets of paper, gliding, penetrating them, metamorphic without mutating, evolving. I perceive it as full and slow, expansive, and at the same time on the verge of disappearing, already ghostly.

What happens in this use of color, in this oscillation that goes from the density of the pigment to a luminous cloud of a halo, leads to a shift to a different way of seeing, to the acceptance of detachment, of the disappearance of forms, but also to the acceptance of undecidability, indeterminacy, unpredictability. My intuition tells me that the image is there, in the radiant thickness of this floating line, at this porous edge, at this changeable, versatile border between abstraction—I stand before movements, forces, impulses, currents, presences—and figuration—I stand before landscapes, clearings, skies, dawns, fires, perhaps twilights, I stand before the dew of a winter meadow, con-densation in a whisky glass, an evening sea, a cloudy sky, a ghostly love. I stand before absence, before something that is happening and that I do not know. What happens to us when we disappear. Disappearance.

Claire Chesnier remains at a distance, observing the emptiness, her language plays in the si-lence, clear, waiting, while she is a replica of her color, which enters into the whiteness of the paper, carrying it without forcing it, becoming one with the paper in the streaks that remain, the smoothness of a current, the suggestion of evaporation.

We look, and it is like a conversation, like taking up a language: our eyes are our mouths, our movements are like sentences, and soon only time is left—the time of painting, which is the time of looking. Then the words try something, venture out and create a terrain where painting and literature draw from the same language. But even more than a common lexicon, it is above all the fact that we speak to each other *"by resonance, by ricochet"* that allows us to enter into dialogue: the fact that, as Claire Chesnier writes, we deposit *"images with words, throw small pebbles on the surface of the water to create circles and see how they grow and spread on the surface in concentric waves."* In the encounter, a language is formed that resembles the great work of the imagination, like a long dance that brings together affects and dura-tions, sensations and the forgotten, a detail and a practice, texts, including those of the poets, painters and philosophers that travel through

*Fragments d'une déposition,*[2] reminding us that each work is based on other works. I listen, her voice echoes in the studio: grain, tempo, cadence, inflection, silence, momentum, tension between precision and fluctuation of meaning, hers. Her sentence is like a gesture.

2. All quotes by Claire Chesnier are taken from her book *Fragments d'une déposition* (forthcoming).

The sheets of paper lie flush against the walls, I approach them, look at them, but there is nothing to see and everything to feel. The object has left the painted surface, it has emptied the space, the subject has dissolved, atomized, disintegrated, so much so that each work seems to me like a wave without beginning or end, a space where representations take shape and are distorted, the place of availability and pure becoming, of the infinite repetition of the gesture, similar and different each time. And now, slightly distanced, with my back to the large table in the center, I feel a little dizzy: that each work can simultaneously evoke a suspension of meaning and an expansion of subjectivity—projection, interpretation, emotion.

When does the word "patience" come to my mind? I begin to move and the pictures vibrate around us, fluttering in chromatic instability, almost the same, essentially the same, in this vertical format that is proportional to the body, or rather to the body of the artist, as she writes in *Fragments d'une déposition: "My height, my shoulder, the extent and fullness of my arm movements correspond to the dimensions of the paper. I cut it to my size—the size of a woman. The horizon of the frame is thus drawn in this perceived space, in my scale..."* Images that suddenly seem to encompass her completely, to regain their character of portraits—self-portraits.

I hear the word *patience* in this endless movement back to the paper, this bending of the upper body, this tension in the neck, this stretching of the arm, this letting go of the wrist. A subterranean tension that responds to the body, to pain, but also to pleasure. That repeats, starts again, returns, works to elicit meaning from the image, to reduce its complexity, to distill the smallest, most insignificant grain, in an effort to cancel out any motif, any intentionality. This persistence in painting. Patience as *insistence*, as *resistance*. Patience, silent and rebellious.

When I think about it, I probably felt this word in connection with that of *confidence*, of trust, which comes to mind at the same time. Having confidence in painting, relying on it, completely, accepting it without hesitation; letting go of control and reaffirming one's instinct, *"to be almost a beginner in the context of painting, but without being careless. It has nothing to do with knowledge, but with allowing oneself the wonder of the ordinary, and sometimes of a fleeting disruption."* And no doubt I understand it, this word, through that of *alliance*, which is also in my head. Patience in alliance with time, *endurance*. A willingness to merge with the flow of life, to make a pact with time, to desire what is to come—*amor fati*—that crosses landscapes, breathes, travels far.

The sheets of paper are suspended, meaning is suspended, language is suspended, time is suspended, and the city pulsates around us as I discover this activation of abandonment—the impossible event that took place here. A painting of patience.

176 × 136 cm

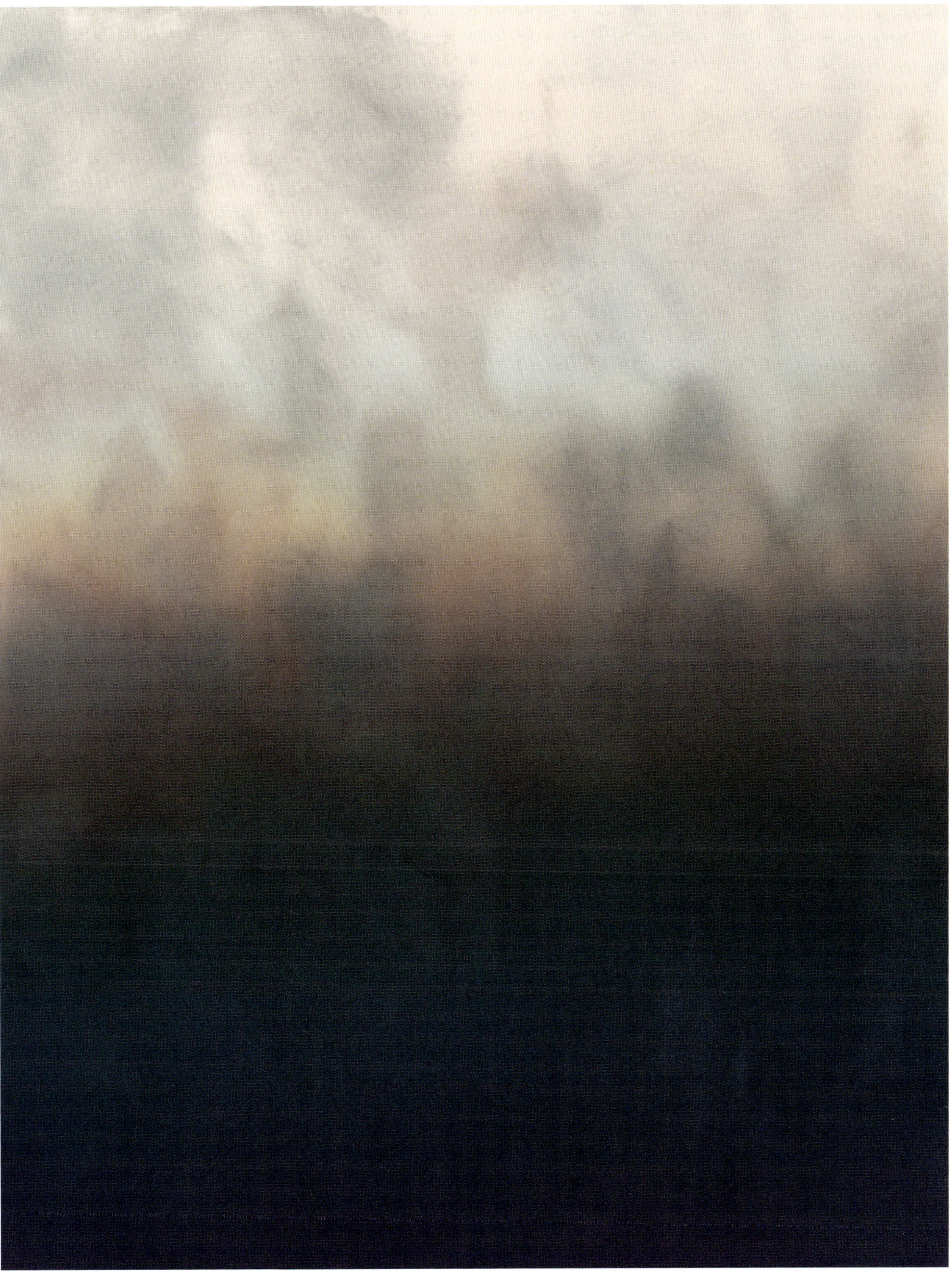

144,5 × 135,5 cm

74

← **110524**     165 × 136 cm     2024
← **111123**     162,5 × 135,5 cm     2023
→ **131022**     171 × 136 cm     2022

168,5 × 135 cm

173 × 136 cm

92

←010223                          172 × 135 cm                          2023
←070223                          173 × 136 cm                          2023
→070224                          170 × 136 cm                          2024

| ← **010224** | 136 × 111 cm | 2024 |
| ← **110324** | 128 × 108 cm | 2024 |
| → **030324** | 171 × 136 cm | 2024 |

→ **120523** 172,5 × 137 cm 2023
↘ **270123** 170 × 135,5 cm 2023
↘ **010922** 170 × 135 cm 2022

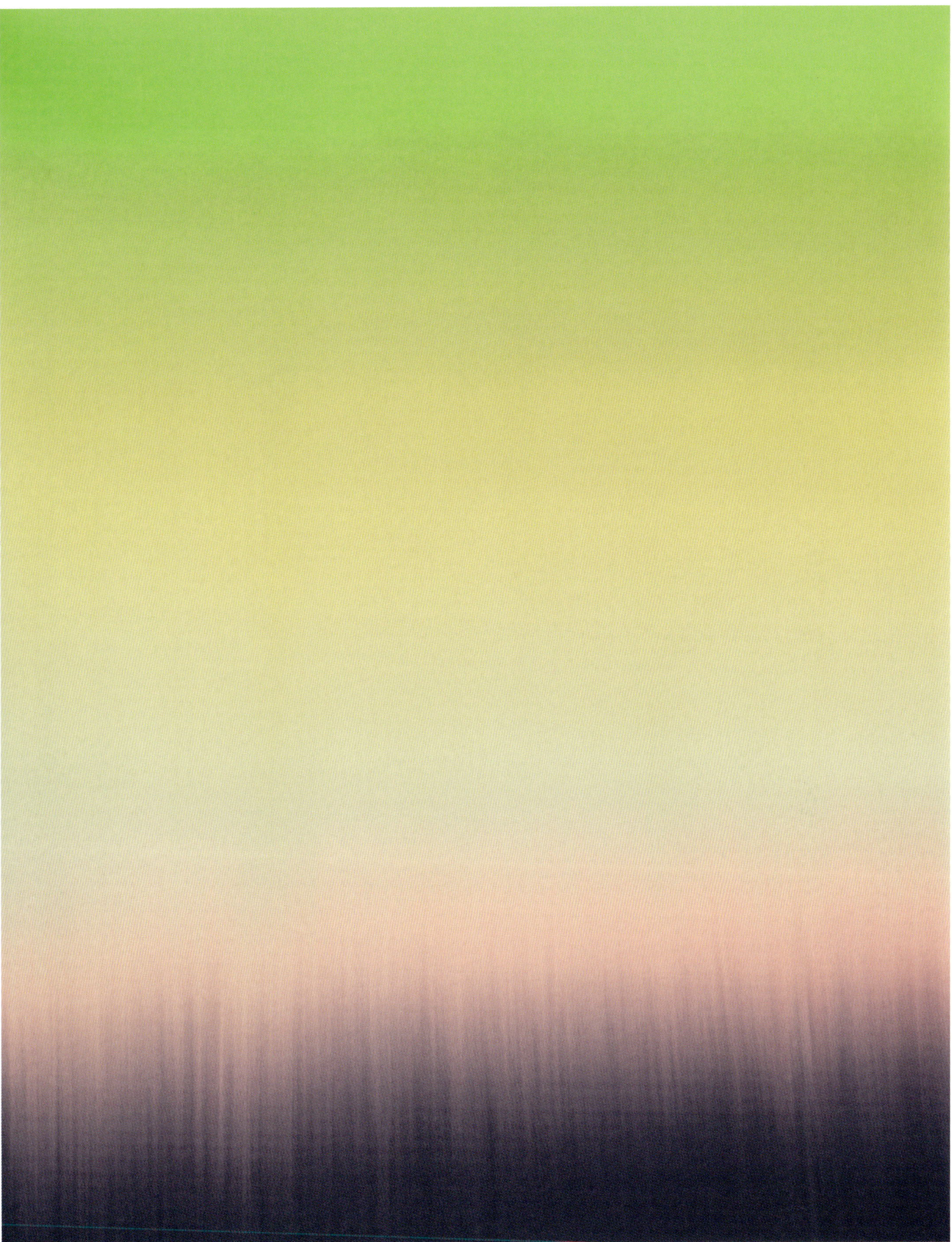

**OUTSIDE: THE ART
OF CLAIRE CHESNIER**
MOLLY WARNOCK

Each new work in the distinctive painterly medium Claire Chesnier has developed begins with the preparation of the paper support. A roughly life-size expanse is cut from a longer roll, affixed to hardboard, and moistened, a step that requires the utmost care: Opening the paper fibers, it makes the surface more vulnerable to the pressure of the artist's touch. Next, she mixes large quantities of pigments, diluting a range of dense calligraphy inks with considerable amounts of water. Proceeding intuitively, with the support in an upright position, she brings one highly liquid hue after another to the paper, depositing it there with a loaded brush. The process is at once immersive and physically extenuating, and the painting of a single work can take up to several weeks. Each is titled after its date of completion—for example: *090324* for a painting finished on March 9, 2024. All are mounted on Dibond and framed prior to exhibition.

Particularly in recent years, the results unmistakably conjure the conventions of landscape painting. Lighter veils of color—often nacre, bluish, or roseate in effect—frequently occupy the upper registers, while darker tones are reserved for the lower reaches. The transitions within these respective zones are extraordinarily subtle, even infinitesimal, whereas the liminal areas between them engage bolder contrasts suggesting so many horizons. The thresholds are at times nearly level across the painting's width; elsewhere, in the works Chesnier informally refers to as "chevrons"—nomenclature doubtless inspired by the more recent history of color field painting, Kenneth Noland's in particular—the darker region slopes upward to either lateral edge in a V-shape. In no case, however, does the seam appear a clearly demarcated line. Rather, the downward flow of ink consistently leaves behind long striations that, in turn, similarly permit reading in naturalistic terms—as long grasses, say, or distant trees backlit by a setting or rising sun. Such associations are nonetheless unmoored by the fluid handling of the whole: There are no securely graspable things; indeed, there are no *things* at all.

Chesnier, for her part, readily avows her feeling for the long tradition of landscape depiction and atmospheric observation, from the nineteenth-century cloud studies of John Constable and the plein-air beach scenes of Eugène Boudin to the invented seascapes of the contemporary Brazilian painter Lucas Arruda. Yet her paintings do not originate in representational intent, and they cannot be understood simply as vestigial variations on a storied genre. They emerge, rather, from her embodied experience of painting—and the spatial, or indeed place-making, possibilities of color.

■■■

In the first compositions in dilute ink on paper that Chesnier exhibited publicly, and which she created between 2010 and 2012, color appears doubly circumscribed. It is confined, first, to a clearly delimited area within the support, the artist having masked the margins prior to applying the ink. Hemmed in by white space, the forms consistently resist appearing deduced from the painting's framing edges, eschewing rectilinearity and symmetry in favor of more idiosyncratic, off-kilter silhouettes. That preliminary shaping is in turn prolonged and displaced by the division of color within the painted zones. Here too, different hues are apportioned in ways that suggest a certain willfulness with respect to preexisting edges (in this case, the internal frame formed by masking): Curves are pitted against angles, plumb lines against gentle swells. The bounds between adjacent color areas are often considerably sharper than in the later paintings, and the results admit various associations, including eccentric shields in the larger works and eyes or fans in the smaller formats.

Over the course of 2012, much of this internal drawing falls away in favor of consistently vertical veils, as if Chesnier's glowing color were dissolving its own boundaries from within. She nonetheless continues to selectively mask the supports, a gesture she now describes as "authoritarian"—an imposition of limits visibly at odds with the inherent fluidity of her medium. This tension is integral to Chesnier's most sustained group of paintings with shaped areas, which she unofficially designates as "blades" (*lames*). Produced between 2013 and 2016 in both small and large formats, these works are characterized by intensely saturated and internally variegated forms that appear simultaneously to be cut out from, and yet dynamically cleaving, their otherwise pristine white grounds. The shapes never recur exactly from one work to another but are instead stretched or attenuated, brought closer to the framing bounds or pulled back from them anew. The very longevity of this painting group suggests the depth of Chesnier's attachment to this preparatory definition, the formal effects of which oscillate, paradoxically, between quasi-sculptural carving and something akin to photographic cropping.

By contrast, the works Chesnier began making later in 2016 give full reign to fluidity. Color ceases to be confined to a specific zone within the paper and instead occupies the totality of the surface, interrupted only by the framing edges.[1] Or to put the same point a slightly different way: Shaping is confined to the inaugural determination of the work's dimensions. That decision remains residually "subjective." Unlike other artists she admires, such as Agnes Martin or Ad Reinhardt, Chesnier does not have a standard format but, rather, subtly alters at least one variable—height or breadth—from one work to the

1. Two distinct groups of smaller paintings, from 2013 and 2016, seem to have played an especially important role in preparing this shift to edge-to-edge veils: In both bodies of work, the blade-like forms are at once more nearly rectilinear and more consistently trued and fared to the framing edges, though they remain set off by stark white margins of varied widths.

next. Just as she had previously adjusted the discrete forms within the fields, never precisely repeating any given silhouette, so she conceives each painting as a specific physical entity. Yet this shaping is determinedly minimal, almost self-effacingly conventional, by contrast with the earlier masking. In another important shift, the paintings are from this moment forward consistently life-size: Initially comparable to the final large-scale blades, which tended to be between 140 and 155 centimeters tall and approximately 135 centimeters wide, they have over the years increased gradually in height, and are now likely to run between 165 and 175 centimeters along the vertical axis.[2]

Within these newly immersive fields, the landscape-like disposition emerges gradually.[3] One discerns a lightening, at first primarily in the paintings' uppermost reaches, then creeping downward; the lower regions darken as if in response. That darkening is also, increasingly, a grounding or weighting, a perception further enhanced by the sedimented trails of downward-flowing ink. These paintings are visibly pulled by gravity, throughout their making as in their eventual hanging. The color veils, meanwhile, span the surface in increasingly regular side-to-side arrays, nearly identical—but never quite—to left and right.

Yet precisely these same recurrent features might be seen as at least equally attuned to the upright human body: its bilateral symmetry, its headedness and its handedness, its verticality and its groundedness.[4] The horizon, on this view, functions less as a representational device than as an index of bodily orientation and equilibrium, situating the beholder squarely before the work.[5] Further underscoring their rootedness in embodied experience, these paintings disclose slight but significant asymmetries. The darker, lower zone often rises slightly higher toward one or the other lateral edge, most often the right—an effect recurrent across the thresholds but perhaps most apparent in the chevrons. The propensity calls to mind the lived difference between our right and left limbs and, more especially, our dominant and non-dominant hands. Far from providing views on a world indifferently spread out before us, Chesnier's paintings suggest the primordial entanglement of body and place. Or perhaps: they refigure embodiment *as* spaciousness—opening and extension.

∎∎∎

The co-emergence or, as he would say, "compearance" of body and place is a central theme in the writings of Jean-Luc Nancy. The key text is *Corpus*, an acknowledged reference for Chesnier. A sustained rethinking of the body inherited in part from Maurice Merleau-

2. It is telling that, beginning with her move to edge-to-edge color veils, Chesnier's formats are sorted by medium distinctions. Previously, the artist had made paintings in ink on paper at a range of dimensions, from the very small (formats she would describe as scaled to the face) to the nearly life-size (that is, scaled to the body). Following the abandonment of masking, by contrast, inks are deployed exclusively on large-format papers, whereas smaller dimensions are reserved for monotypes in lithographic ink or, more recently, colored pencils. Not incidentally, the headedness and handedness effects I describe below as defining of the large inks on paper tend to be mitigated in the smaller works in other media, which result from a different bodily relationship to their maker.

3. More precisely, this aspect *re-emerges*, for the painted zones in many blades similarly register as landscape-like, suggesting views through various apertures. But that resonance appears momentarily scrambled by the qualitative leap to the edge-to-edge works, after which it assumes newfound potency—or so I wish to suggest.

4. The terms "headedness" and "handedness" figure centrally in my account of related effects in the abstract paintings of James Bishop, an artist Chesnier admires; see my "Field Agent: The Art of James Bishop," *Artforum* 52:5 (January 2014): 184-89, 234. My discussion here is also indebted to Michael Fried's "Orientation in Painting: Caspar David Friedrich," in idem., *Another Light: Jacques-Louis David to Thomas Demand* (New Haven and London: Yale University Press, 2014): 111-49.

5. For a related discussion, see Briony Fer's account of what she characterizes as the "seam" or "hinge" between the upper and lower zones in Mark Rothko's late black-and-gray paintings in idem., "Seeing in the Dark," in Achim Borchardt-Hume, *Rothko: The Late Series* (London: Tate Modern, 2008), especially 42-43.

Ponty's phenomenology, *Corpus* invites us to confront anew the Cartesian conception of the *res extensa*. In Nancy's telling, the body is not indifferently dropped into space, for there is no homogeneous, infinite space; rather, there are only the spaces or indeed *places* that bodies bring forth: "Bodies aren't some kind of fullness or filled space (space is filled everywhere): they are *open* space, implying, in some sense, a space more properly *spacious* than spatial, what could also be called a *place*. Bodies are places of existence, and nothing exists without a place, a *there*, a 'here,' a 'here is,' for a *this*."[6]

Of special interest here is Nancy's account of the Cartesian "*ego sum, ego existo*": the declaration of existence. Nancy frames that affirmation as a rupture or breakthrough. Yet he also stresses the finitude of the enunciation, its contingency upon discrete circumstance. The ego is at once localized and drawn beyond itself—"'ego' being 'ego' only when articulated, articulating itself as spacing or flexion, even the inflexion of a site."[7] For precisely this reason, he suggests, such proffering is necessarily iterative, indeed interminable: "For prof-fering 'ego' (for thrusting it outside the self, so that there might be a 'self'), all places are equally effective, but only as places... I am, every time I am, the flexion of a place, a fold or motion through which it prof-fers (itself)."[8] We have to do here not with an ego "in" a body, but with the necessarily embodied being of ego: what Nancy calls "*corpus ego*."[9]

Nancy's claim that such articulation "happens ceaselessly, every time, in every space of time, in every moment of existing" offers a way of thinking about the simultaneous discreteness and enchainment of Chesnier's paintings, features we are perhaps more accustomed to describing in terms of the broadly serial impetus of painting since Impressionism.[10] Their titling resembles the dating of journal entries, yet the works themselves are resolutely stripped of autobiographical anecdote—indeed, of the conventional painterly hallmarks of authorial presence (emphatic brushwork, impasto, pentimenti...). Certain works produced in quick succession suggest quasi-cinematic sequences: for example, a cluster of works produced between late January and early February 2022 (*280122, 020222, 040222,* and *060222*) evoking a gradual pan across gently sloping but essentially nondescript, if not desolate, terrain ("all places are equally effective..."). Even so, each painting within this group is clearly set off from the others. From one work to the next, minimal tonal variations within a largely shared and relatively sober palette evoke so many distinctions in their internal weather—differences, as it were, of perceived humidity or pressure or temperature, less seen than sensed.[11] Elsewhere, by contrast, the decalage between chronologically consecutive paintings is immediately striking. Consider *010922* and *020922*, completed on the first and second days,

6. Jean-Luc Nancy, *Corpus*, trans. Richard A. Rand (New York: Fordham University Press, 2008), 15.

7. Ibid., 25.

8. Ibid., 27.

9. Ibid., 25.

10. Ibid. Chesnier, notably, does not consider her work serial, preferring to speak of painting "families" within her corpus (conversation with the author, March 2024).

11. In an interview, Chesnier states that her works are inevitably permeated by the weather proper to the time and place of their making (or as Nancy might put it, the fleeting conditions of the *ego sum, ego existo*): "My painting is very closely related to certain qualities of temperature, of climate, of color... The relationship is nearly Impressionist... But it's a connection made after the fact"—a matter, one might say, of something nearer to infiltration than to conscious intent (Thomas Lévy-Lasne, "Les Apparences, épisode 19: Claire Chesnier" [October 2021]. This characterization does not come down clearly on either side of the abstraction/figuration binary as conventionally understood, and indeed, Chesnier is largely uninterested in this distinction, declaring her relationship to these categories "very, very fluid" (conversation with the author, July 2024).

respectively, of September 2022. The former ranges from vivid chartreuse in the upper register to deep purple in the lowest reaches; the latter, from saturated vermillion to subdued veridian. The change in feeling is total, even as the two works are clearly related by their atypically low horizons. This is another variety of continuity-in-difference.

In Chesnier's paintings, articulation is entirely an affair of color, in its bottomless singularity and inherent plurality. The artist has spoken of the "haptic charge" where colors touch, and that touching takes place at another limit, that of the support itself. Color, here—and here, and here, and there...—is no longer *formed*; rather, it is delivered into the spacing, folding, or flexion proper to a *place*. Notably, in her private notebooks, the artist prolongs this articulation by attempting to name the new hues that emerge from the painting process—a theoretically interminable re-wording.

■■■

For many readers, this account of Chesnier's work and thought will already have conjured Supports/Surfaces, the volatile and shifting collective of painters—Louis Cane, Daniel Dezeuze, Marc Devade, and Claude Viallat, among others—active in France in the late 1960s and 70s. In her work, as in theirs, one discerns a clear visual relationship to aspects of post-WWII American abstraction—in particular, in Chesnier's case, the vertically stacked color blocks of Mark Rothko, the poured veils of Morris Louis, the stripe and chevron paintings of Kenneth Noland, and the sprayed fields of Jules Olitski. And she, too, understands color as inextricably bound in larger questions about subjectivity and the body—issues the Supports/Surfaces painters and their critical champions once argued had been effectively banished from the more "positivist" orientation of American high modernism.[12] Her engagement with Nancy's thinking extends this filiation: Writers in the Supports/Surfaces milieu at times referred explicitly to the early work of Nancy's later interlocutor and collaborator Jacques Derrida—most notably, his assertion that "the chromatic... is to the origin of art what writing is to speech": that is, that color is an affair of spacing.[13] This conception, as we have seen, lies at the heart of Chesnier's enterprise.

I nonetheless want to close by considering a handful of paintings that bring us back to the specificity of that practice. Beginning in 2016, coincident with her abandonment of masking, Chesnier has occasionally exhibited works that are created and titled in the same way as her edge-to-edge paintings for the wall but then, in an additional step, displaced ninety degrees and displayed horizontally. In selected gallery presentations, the artist has installed such works on pedestals

12. For a detailed account of this reception, see my "*Tel Quel* and the Subject of American Painting: Marcelin Pleynet and James Bishop," *Tate Papers* 32 (December 2019).

13. "*La chromatique, (...) est à l'origine de l'art ce que l'écriture est à la parole.*" This quote, drawn from Derrida's watershed *De la grammatologie* (Of Grammatology), 1967, serves as one of several epigraphs to Marc Devade, "D'une peinture chromatique. Théorème écrit à travers la peinture" (1970), rpt. in Camille Saint-Jacques, ed., *Marc Devade. Écrits théoriques* (Paris: Lettres Modernes, 1989): 31-51. For an English version, see "Chromatic Painting: Theorem Written Through Painting," trans. Roland-François Lack, in Patrick Ffrench and Lack, eds., *The Tel Quel Reader* (London and New York: Routledge, 1998): 181-97.

raised sixty centimeters off the ground, perpendicular to her wall-hung paintings along the same sightline.[14] The effect, as captured in installation photographs, resembles a colored fold in three dimensions, the horizontal painting providing something like a runway for the gaze.

Yet the recumbent paintings also carry distinctive connotations. Indelibly inscribed with the traces of their upright origins, they reverse the horizontal-to-vertical trajectory so frequently adopted in painting since Jackson Pollock or, closer to Supports/Surfaces, Simon Hantaï, whose abstractions famously were produced on the floor and rotated to the wall. Chesnier's paintings, by contrast, register as *deposed*—and indeed, she describes them informally as *gisants*, in reference to the sculptural tradition of the sepulchral effigy. But these bodies remain wholly singular, which is to say singularly spaced, in what we are invited to imagine as the horizontal extension of the *here lies*.[15] Prolonging the articulation at work on the walls, they are but further places—further profferings—of finite being.

14. An exception to this staging, displayed much lower to the ground, was the horizontally disposed work Chesnier included in her 2019 contribution to *L'art dans les chapelles*, at the Chapel de la Trinité, Castennec, Bieuzy.

15. I borrow this last bit of phrasing from Nancy, who describes "a writing of the dead having nothing to do with the discourse of Death—only with this fact, that the space of bodies knows no Death (the fantasy of abolished space), but knows each body as a dead one, as *this* dead one, sharing with us the extension of its *here lies*" (*Corpus*, 55). And just here, another comparison comes into view: Yves Klein's *RP3*, "*Ci-gît l'Espace*" (RP3, "Here Lies Space") of 1960, which photographs indicate he displayed on a wall in his studio but exhibited publicly in a horizontal position. The relationship of Chesnier's art to Klein's is a large and rich topic requiring a more detailed analysis than I can provide here; suffice it to say that Klein imagines color—more specifically, intensely saturated monochromy—as a waystation to precisely the infinite, immaterial space Nancy dislocates in favor of discontinuous, heterogeneous *places*.

← 020423      165 × 135 cm      2023
← 030623      172 × 137 cm      2023
→ 130623      172,5 × 136 cm      2023

←**170523**        162 × 136 cm        2023
←**140223**        160 × 134,5 cm        2023
→**300323**        171,5 × 135 cm        2023

← **130424**         161,5 × 135 cm                    2024
← **090424**         170 × 137 cm                      2024
→ **060323**         161,5 × 135,5 cm                  2023

→ **210323** 170,5 × 135 cm 2023
↘ **131023** 161,5 × 135,5 cm 2023
↘ **080923** 162,5 × 136,5 cm 2023

144

172 × 135 cm

154

# THE SKY IS FULL, AND OPENING AGAIN*
## CLAIRE CHESNIER

*This title is a quotation from André du Bouchet's *L'Inhabité*, 1967

In this installation of images and light, painterly and scientific elements come together. Both are linked to the sensory experience of seeing, influenced by the variations in light that shape our perception of a work of art and its surroundings. Paintings have a tactile surface that responds to changes in natural light throughout the day, revealing subtle variations in hue. As engineers at the start-up Olumee, Arnaud Lejeune, Guillaume Lejeune and Jean-Yves Moulin have developed an innovative lighting system that uses sensors to reproduce the sky's fluctuating temperature and color intensity in real time.

The concept was born from a dream—the dream of immersing the viewer in the contemplative experience of painting, of transferring the ever-changing aspects of the sky, the passage of human time and the evolving mood of a day, from sunrise to sunset, onto the painted surface, and of extending this experience onto the viewer's own skin. Because the sky is always around us, it touches our bodies and we are in it. The air changes and with it the luminosity of our skin, the color of our eyes, our perception of the present moment.

So the same work of art would reflect the vast expanse of shadow under a cloudy sky or the fiery glow of the midday sun in August. I wanted to evoke the temporality of the gaze, of the creation of the painting, of the old masters working in dusky chapels or by candlelight, of stained glass or domestic windows. Let each hour, each moment of this journey become movement, become life. In *The Sky Is Full, and Opening Again*, the light gradations of twelve hours of the day condense into twelve minutes, like an ephemeris.

The modulations of light intensity and temperature were conceived as a tableau, moving from the slow rise of dawn to sudden showers, passing clouds and nightfall in relation to the viewer and the paintings themselves. The weather and the passage of time shape our observation of the surface of the painting as it pulsates and transforms. Painting is about touch, about touching and being touched. I hope that this installation opens up the possibility of a sensitive approach to a time that mirrors the sky, which is no longer just above our heads, but in and before our eyes, embedded in the passing veils of color.

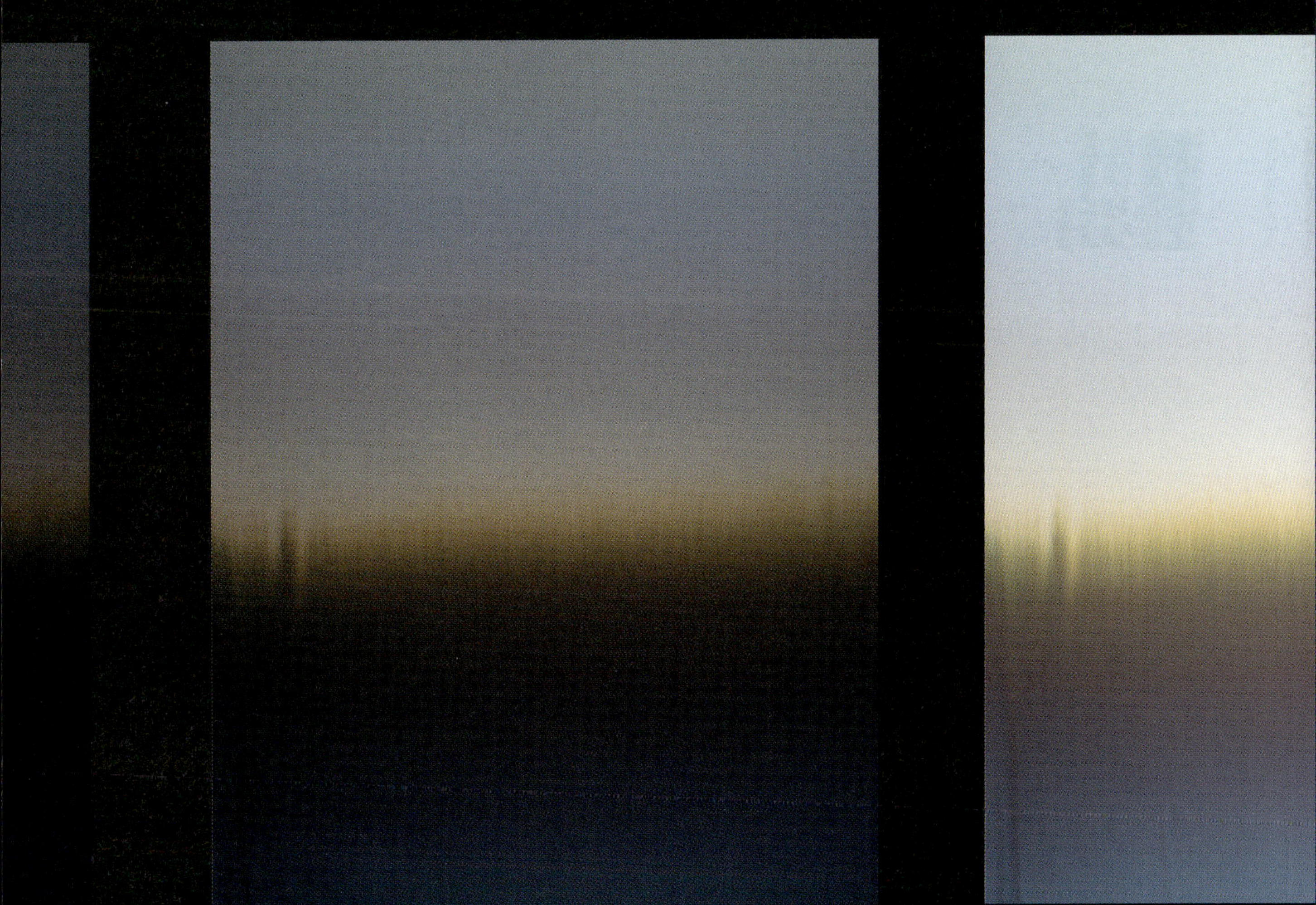

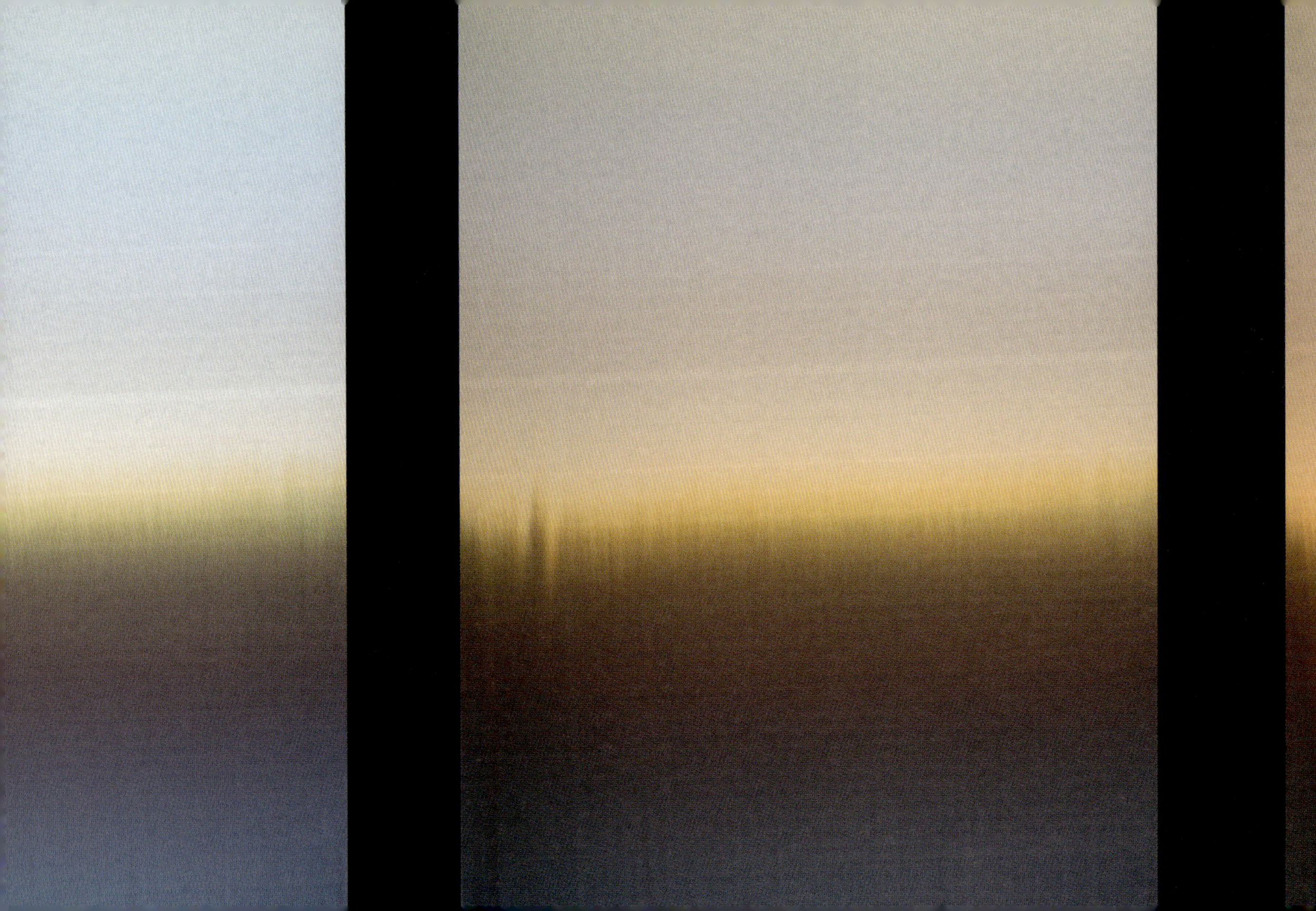

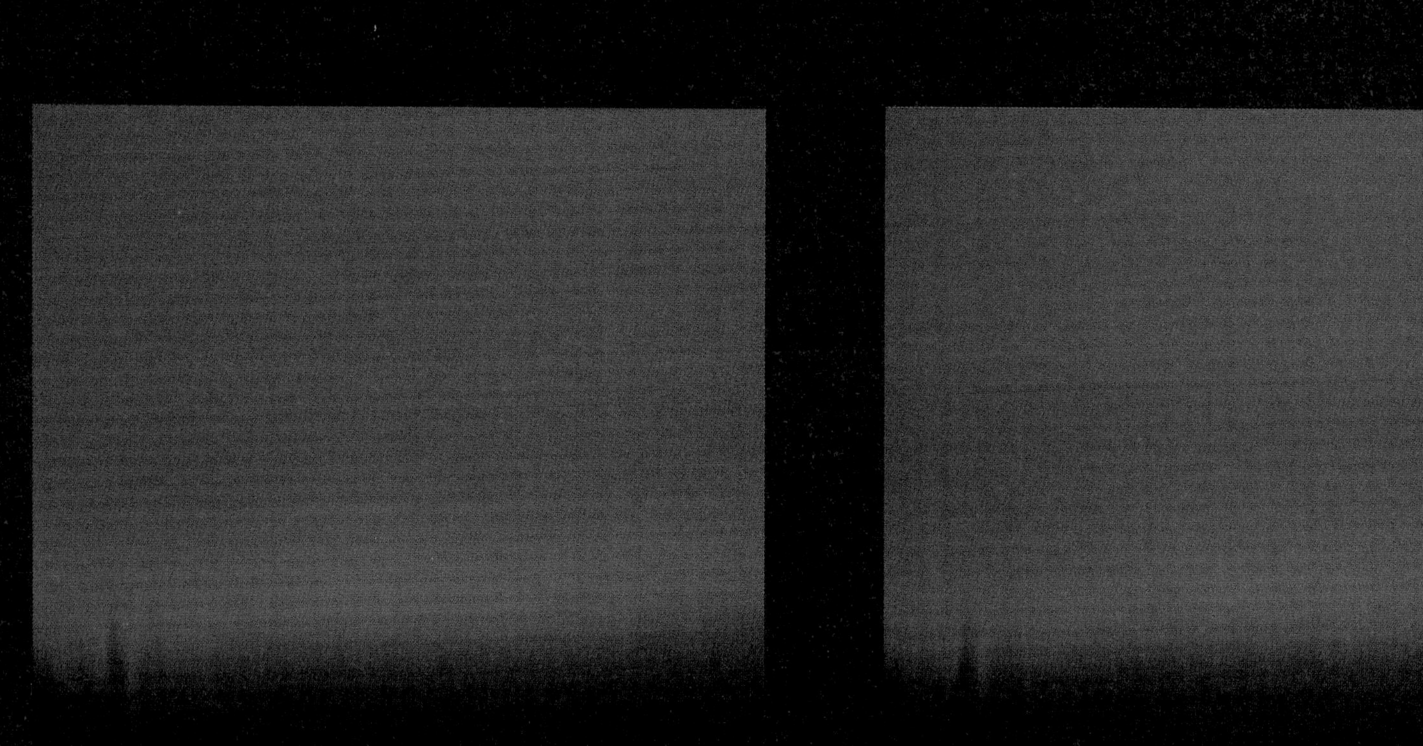

← 230121          41×27 cm          2021
← 060819          41,5×27 cm          2019
→ 030921          46,5×31,5 cm          2021
↘ 171121          46,5×31,5 cm          2021
↘ 141121          46,5×31,5 cm          2021

← 011221          46,5 × 31,5 cm          2021
← 090921          46,5 × 31,5 cm          2021
→ 120519          156 × 133,5 cm          2019

| ← 070319 | 160,5 × 135,5 cm | 2019 |
| ← 011019 | 161 × 134,5 cm | 2019 |
| → 130319 | 172 × 133 cm | 2019 |

← **240521** 158,5 × 105,5 cm 2021
← **270521** 168 × 112 cm 2021
→ **010321** 166 × 135 cm 2021

When I ask her how she paints, Claire Chesnier says that she does not want to answer the question, and prefers to remain silent on the subject. This attitude, apart from her refusal to reduce her art to technical procedures to which too precise an answer would attract undue attention, also says something about the quality of this work: its resistance to unveiling. As indiscreet as my question may seem, given her flat refusal to answer, it remains no less interesting, because this refusal also says something about what her work evokes in me. Why, in front of this work, do I not only want to look, but also to understand? What is it, in the way this painting manifests its presence, that so fascinates me that I want to know what I cannot decipher: the gestures behind such a unique appearance?

To encounter the work of Claire Chesnier is to experience a different kind of presence: something is there, whose presence and impact I perceive without being able to name its nature. It is undoubtedly this tension between the power of this personal encounter, in which the work asserts its uniqueness as a work, and the enigma of its nature, that led me to my question. How can I, in one and the same moment, have the contradictory experience of the obvious and the enigmatic? So when I write about Claire Chesnier, trying to find the right words to describe the ensemble of contradictory sensations, I need to overcome the principle of non-contradiction, which makes us be-lieve that a thing is either this or that. But Claire Chesnier's painting—and this is precisely its essence and singularity—is, at every moment, a way of giving the oxymoron a form that is both visible *and* obvious. Obvious because the first thing that comes to mind, like an observation that only needs to be named, is that *it is there*. And as for what it is...

Let us begin, perhaps, with one of the first sensations: the space here oscillates between two poles, something empathetic that makes you feel as if you could nestle into it; something matte that reminds those who dream of restoring a lost unity, that every painting (even and especially if it is made of paper mounted on Dibond) is a *screen* on which, if you try too hard to get too close to it, you end up missing it. The whole business, the whole work of the artist is to find that rightness, the balance point between depth and screen, just as it is the artist's job to master the fine line between concealing and revealing.

A veil, even more than a painting; her painting is undeniably so because of its ability to create a translucent surface effect, like the fine curtain formed by water in a waterfall. But it is also something else that gives this diaphanous presence its full meaning, far removed from any abstract formalism. As Claire Chesnier puts it, "There must be a body," without which there can be no question of presence. Certainly not a figurative body, for here the figure remains as veiled as the modalities of the artist's practice. But an experienced body: that of the painter as well as that of the person standing in front of the painting. In front of Claire Chesnier's work (and perhaps it is this, after all, the first thing I feel), I have the feeling that I am standing. It is as if the verticality of the work has summoned and made possible my own. It is as if, above all, the way in which the artist has spent hours physically testing the laws of gravity, by accompanying the colored ink on its journey from top to bottom on the support, makes the work the site of a hidden imprint—veil and memory in one.

However, since there is always a *however* in the face of this work, I could write that I am dealing with horizontality when I stand in front of a work by Claire Chesnier. As if, in this liminal space between painted and unpainted, that gradually takes shape as the ink flows downwards, a kind of landscape emerges. To say *landscape* is probably already too much, but what else can I call my feeling? Above all, let us say that there is an expanse here, and that the breath, the rhythm that animates this work, undoubtedly comes from this double play between the verticality of the body and the vastness of the world. Let us say, moreover, that if there is an expanse, then it is cancelled out by the incision that the work makes at the border, a border that is all the sharper for its delicate surface. An expanse contained within a border is what Aristotle defined as a *place*. Voilà, I am standing in front of a place. From now on, it is a question of giving up trying to understand how it came about in order to experience it better.

← CCLXXXVI
→ CCCV

149,8 × 132,4 cm
144 × 133 cm

2014
2015

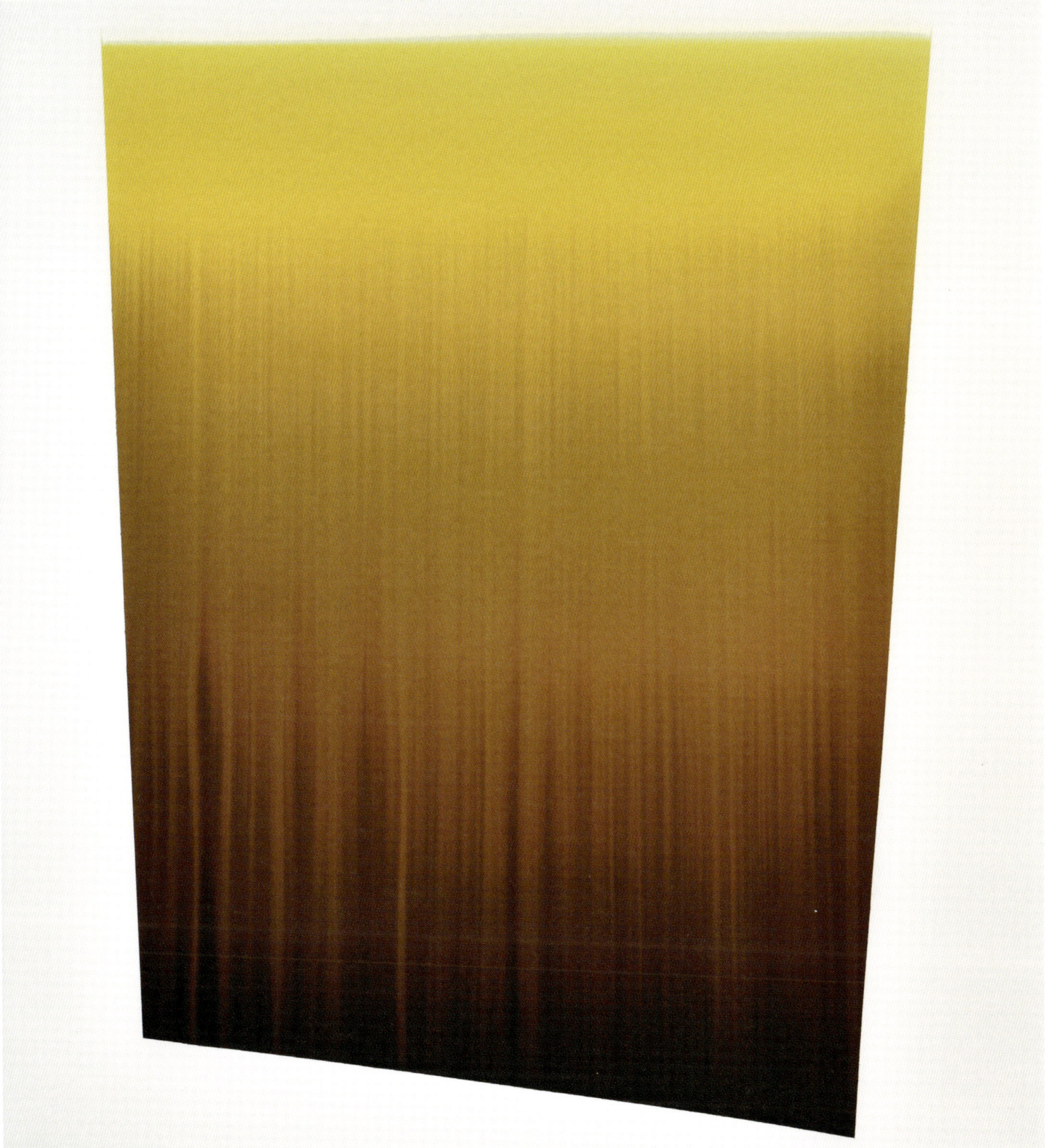

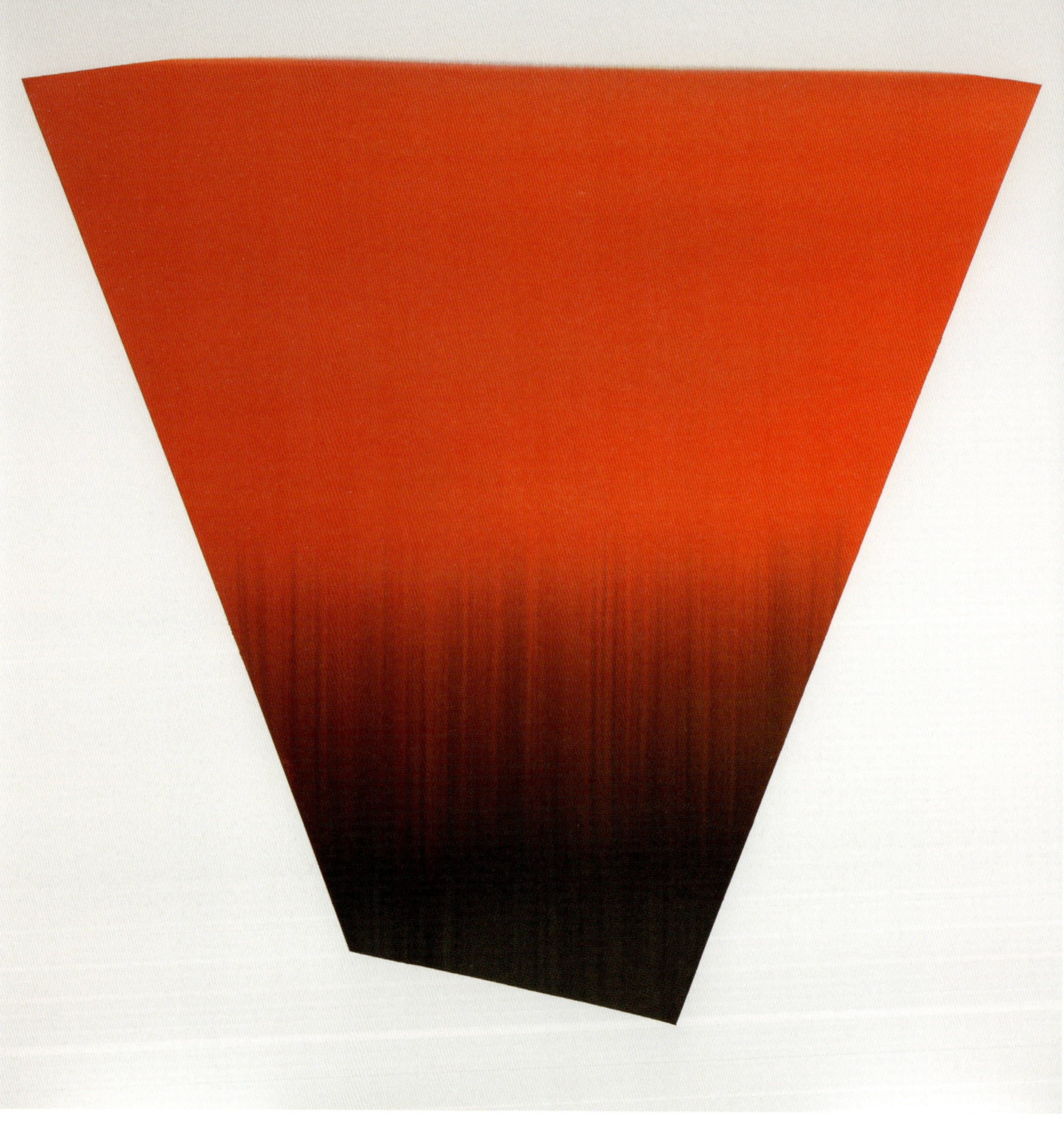

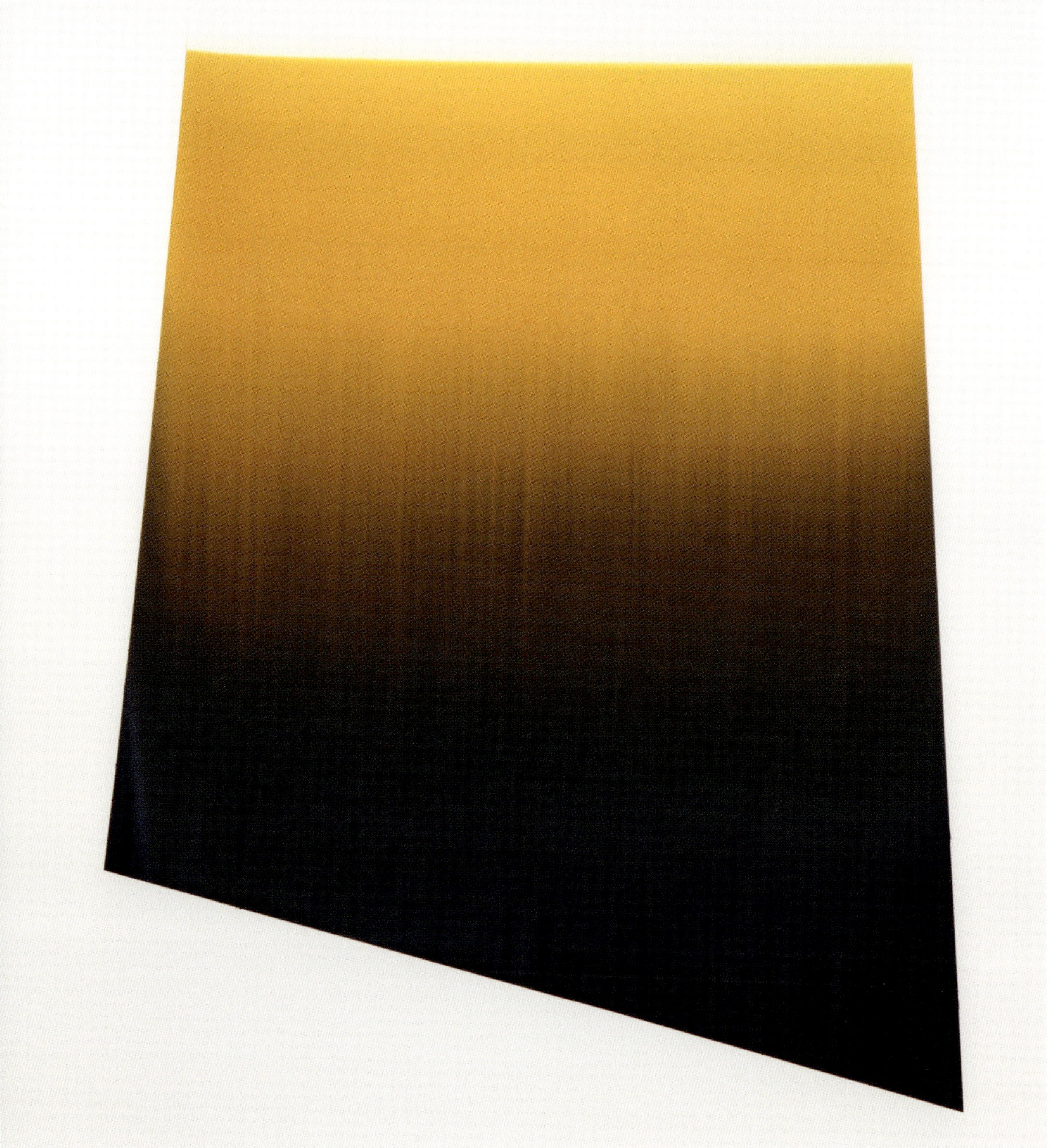

210

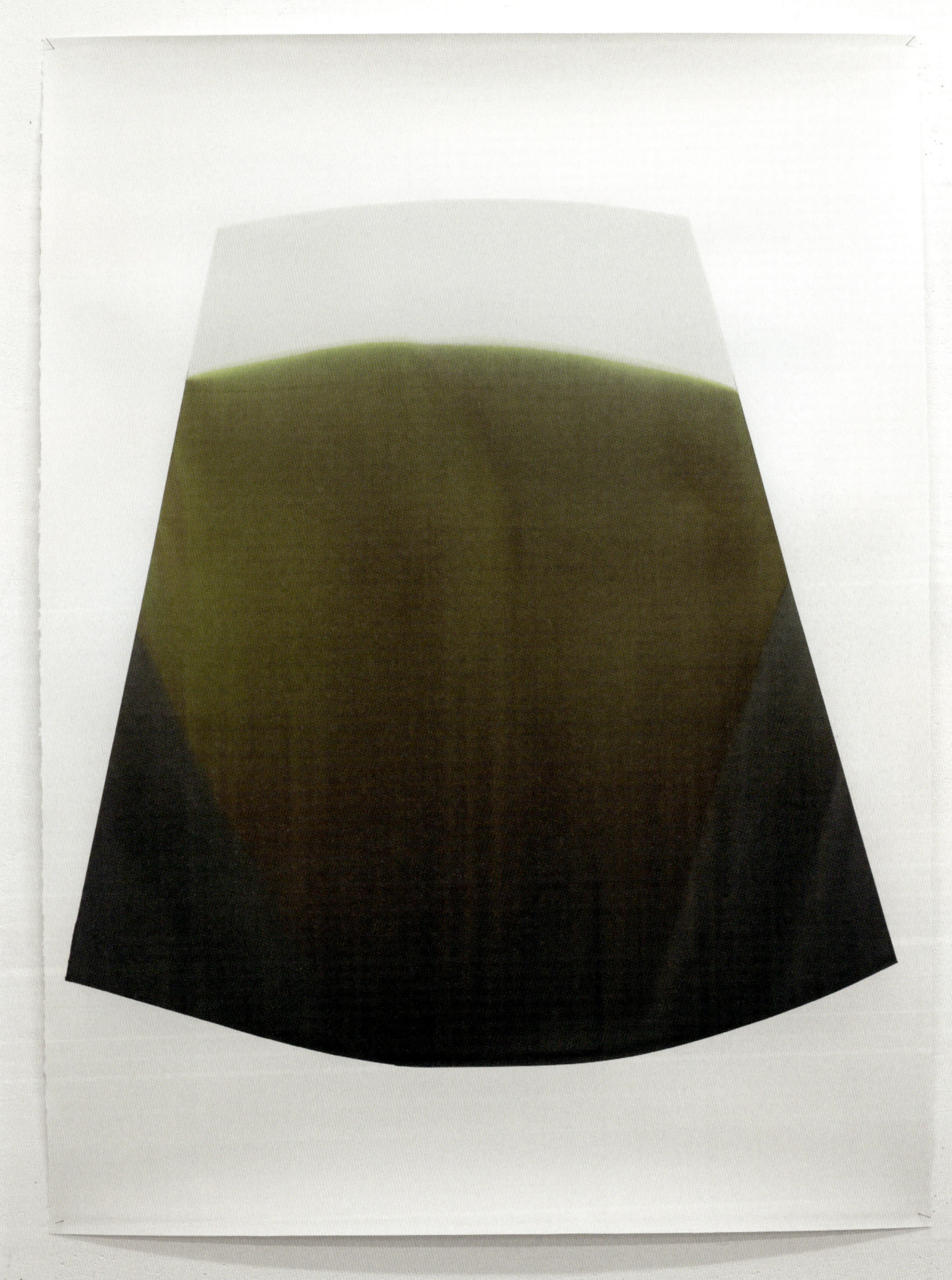

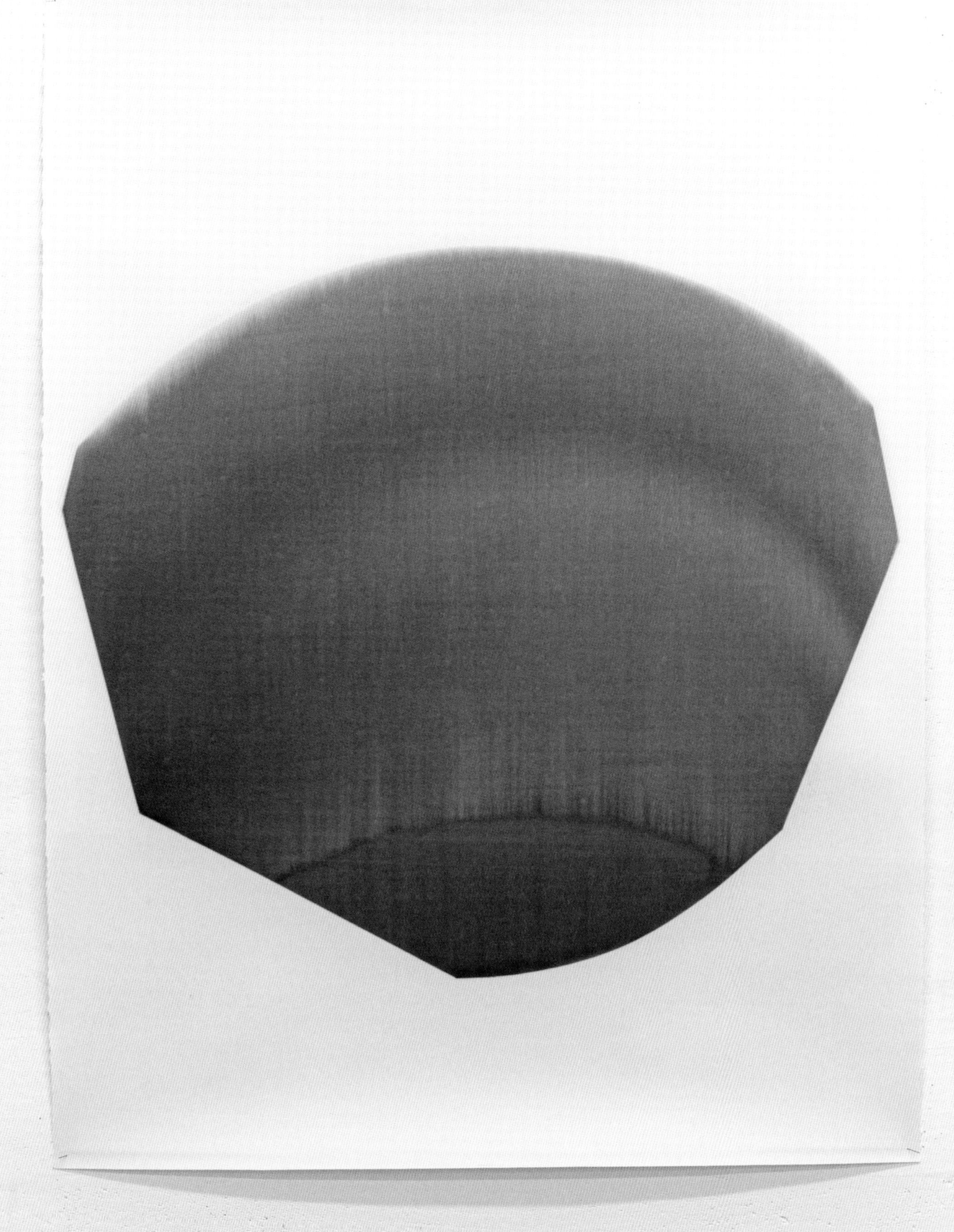

**← CLXIV**  150 × 114 cm  2012
**← CLXVI**  150 × 114 cm  2012
**→ XC**  140 × 114 cm  2010

→ **CXVIII**      150 × 114 cm      2011
↘ **CXC**      147 × 114 cm      2011
↘ **XCVIII**      132 × 114 cm      2010

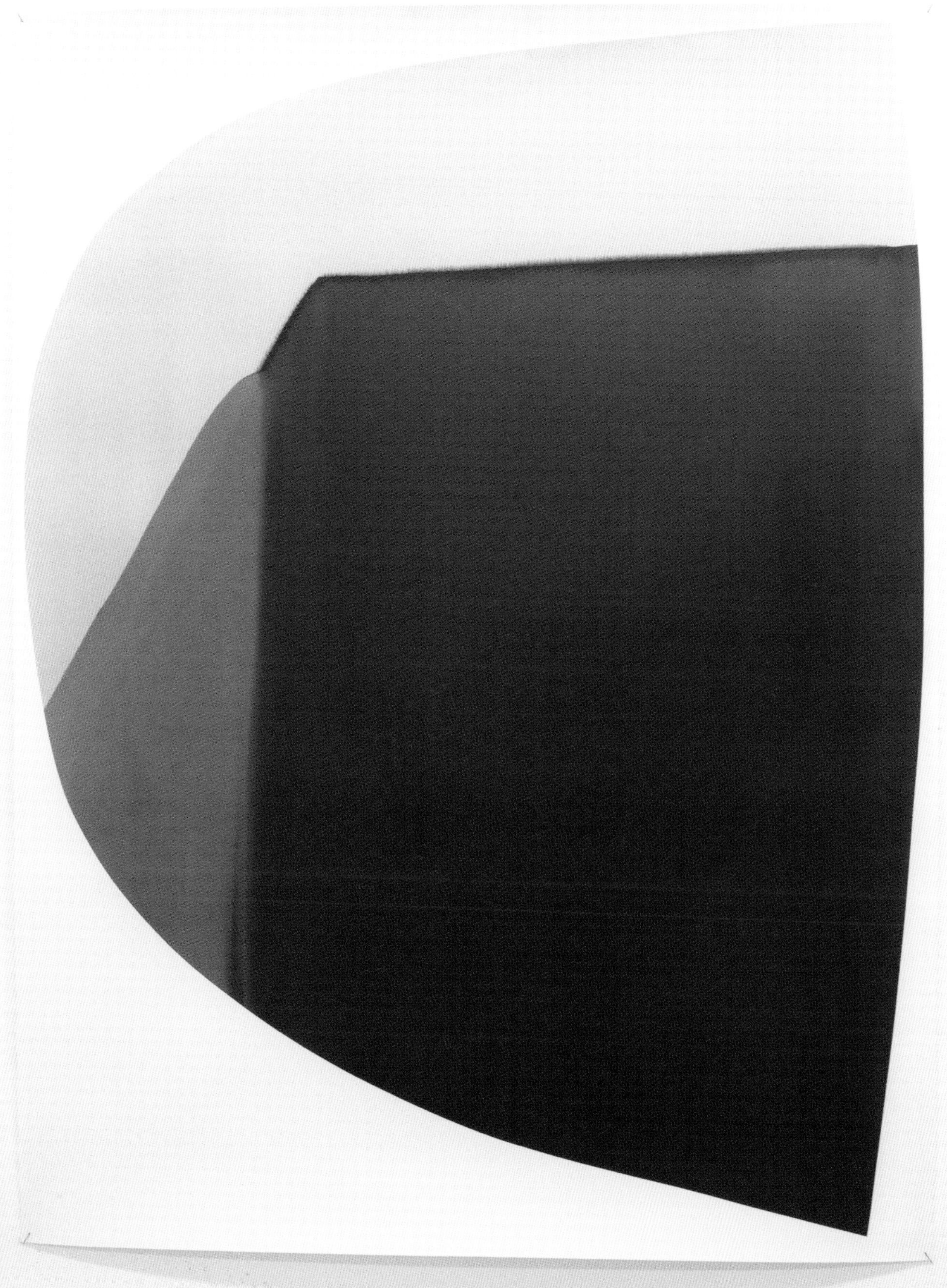

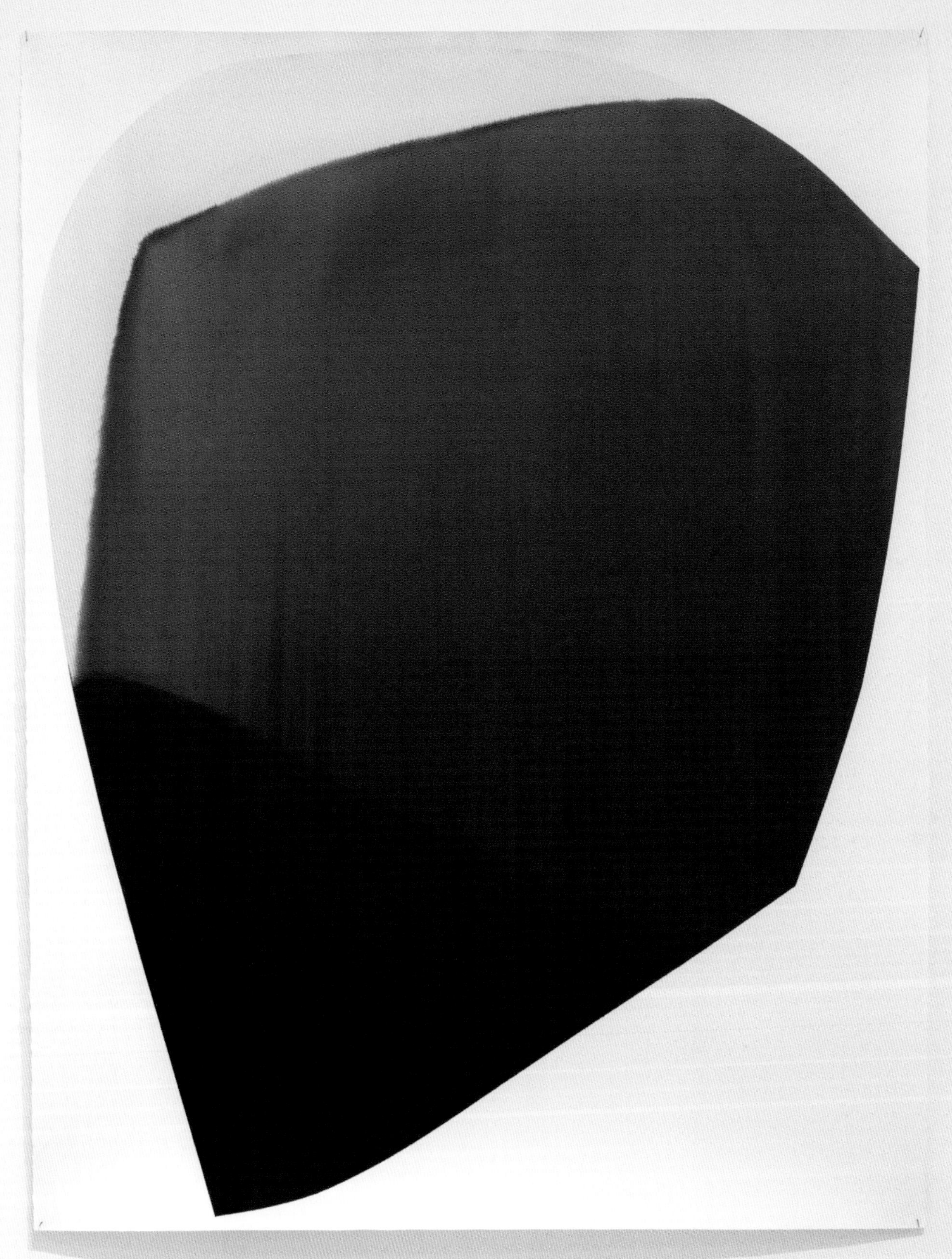

**170624**
172 × 141 cm
ink on paper
2024
Courtesy Ceysson
& Bénétière Gallery
© Fabrice Seixas

**131024**
155 × 135 cm
ink on paper
2024
Courtesy THE PILL®
Gallery
© Fabrice Seixas

**210624**
171 × 142 cm
ink on paper
2024
Courtesy THE PILL®
Gallery
© Fabrice Seixas

**150824**
177 × 141 cm
ink on paper
2024
Courtesy THE PILL®
Gallery
© Fabrice Seixas

**100724**
177 × 136 cm
ink on paper
2024
Courtesy Ceysson
& Bénétière Gallery
© Fabrice Seixas

**091024**
176 × 136 cm
ink on paper
2024
Courtesy THE PILL®
Gallery
© Fabrice Seixas

**231024**
144,5 × 135,5 cm
ink on paper
2024
Courtesy THE PILL®
Gallery
© Fabrice Seixas

**201024**
149 × 134,5 cm
ink on paper
2024
Courtesy THE PILL®
Gallery
© Fabrice Seixas

**140924**
122 × 96,5 cm
ink on paper
2024
Courtesy Ceysson
& Bénétière Gallery
© Fabrice Seixas

**230724**
166 × 137 cm
ink on paper
2024
Courtesy Ceysson
& Bénétière Gallery
© Fabrice Seixas

**280524**
177 × 141 cm
ink on paper
2024
Courtesy THE PILL®
Gallery
© Fabrice Seixas

**200524**
171,5 × 135 cm
ink on paper
2024
Courtesy THE PILL®
Gallery
© Fabrice Seixas

**240524**
170 × 142 cm
ink on paper
2024
Courtesy Ceysson
& Bénétière Gallery
© Fabrice Seixas

**110524**
165 × 136 cm
ink on paper
2024
Private collection
Courtesy Ceysson
& Bénétière Gallery
© Fabrice Seixas

**111123**
162,5 × 135,5 cm
ink on paper
2023
Private collection
Courtesy THE PILL®
Gallery
© Fabrice Seixas

**131022**
171 × 136 cm
ink on paper
2022
Private collection
© Fabrice Seixas

**011222**
168,5 × 135 cm
ink on paper
2022
Courtesy Ceysson
& Bénétière Gallery
© Fabrice Seixas

**270424**
173 × 136 cm
ink on paper
2024
Courtesy Ceysson
& Bénétière Gallery
© Fabrice Seixas

**161222**
171 × 136 cm
ink on paper
2022
Private collection
Courtesy Ceysson
& Bénétière Gallery
© Cyrille Cauvet

**151222**
171 × 135 cm
ink on paper
2022
Private collection
Courtesy THE PILL®
Gallery
© Fabrice Seixas

**010323**
171 × 135 cm
ink on paper
2023
Courtesy Ceysson
& Bénétière Gallery
© Fabrice Seixas

**101222**
165 × 134,5 cm
ink on paper
2022
Courtesy THE PILL®
Gallery
© Fabrice Seixas

**070623**
163 × 136,5 cm
ink on paper
2023
Courtesy THE PILL®
Gallery
© Fabrice Seixas

**010223**
172 × 135 cm
ink on paper
2023
Private collection
Courtesy Ceysson
& Bénétière Gallery
© Cyrille Cauvet

**070223**
173 × 136 cm
ink on paper
2023
Private collection
Courtesy Ceysson
& Bénétière Gallery
© Cyrille Cauvet

**070224**
170 × 136 cm
ink on paper
2024
Courtesy THE PILL®
Gallery
© Nazlı Erdemirel

**300623**
172 × 136 cm
ink on paper
2023
Courtesy Ceysson
& Bénétière Gallery
© Cyrille Cauvet

**010224**
136 × 111 cm
ink on paper
2024
Private collection
Courtesy THE PILL®
Gallery
© Fabrice Seixas

**110324**
128 × 108 cm
ink on paper
2024
Courtesy THE PILL®
Gallery
© Fabrice Seixas

**030324**
171 × 136 cm
ink on paper
2024
Courtesy Ceysson
& Bénétière Gallery
© Fabrice Seixas

**300523**
171,5 × 135,5 cm
ink on paper
2023
Private collection
Courtesy Ceysson
& Bénétière Gallery
© Cyrille Cauvet

**120523**
172,5 × 137 cm
ink on paper
2023
Private collection
Courtesy Ceysson
& Bénétière Gallery
© Cyrille Cauvet

**270123**
170 × 135,5 cm
ink on paper
2023
Private collection
Courtesy Ceysson
& Bénétière Gallery
© Cyrille Cauvet

**010922**
170 × 135 cm
ink on paper
2022
Private collection
Courtesy Ceysson
& Bénétière Gallery
© Cyrille Cauvet

**020423**
165 × 135 cm
ink on paper
2023
Courtesy THE PILL®
Gallery
© Fabrice Seixas

**030623**
172 × 137 cm
ink on paper
2023
Courtesy THE PILL®
Gallery
© Fabrice Seixas

**130623**
172,5 × 136 cm
ink on paper
2023
Courtesy Ceysson
& Bénétière Gallery
© Fabrice Seixas

**170523**
162 × 136 cm
ink on paper
2023
Courtesy Ceysson
& Bénétière Gallery
© Fabrice Seixas

**140223**
160 × 134,5 cm
ink on paper
2023
Courtesy THE PILL®
Gallery
© Fabrice Seixas

**300323**
171,5 × 135 cm
ink on paper
2023
Courtesy Ceysson
& Bénétière Gallery
© Fabrice Seixas

**130424**
161,5 × 135 cm
ink on paper
2024
Courtesy Ceysson
& Bénétière Gallery
© Fabrice Seixas

**090424**
170 × 137 cm
ink on paper
2024
Courtesy Ceysson
& Bénétière Gallery
© Fabrice Seixas

**060323**
161,5 × 135,5 cm
ink on paper
2023
Courtesy Ceysson
& Bénétière Gallery
© Fabrice Seixas

**300423**
164 × 136,5 cm
ink on paper
2023
Courtesy THE PILL®
Gallery
© Fabrice Seixas

**210323**
170,5 × 135 cm
ink on paper
2023
Courtesy THE PILL®
Gallery
© Fabrice Seixas

**131023**
161,5 × 135,5 cm
ink on paper
2023
Courtesy THE PILL®
Gallery
© Fabrice Seixas

**080923**
162,5 × 136,5 cm
ink on paper
2023
Courtesy THE PILL®
Gallery
© Fabrice Seixas

**270422**
171 × 136,5 cm
ink on paper
2022
Private collection
Courtesy Ceysson
& Bénétière Gallery
© Cyrille Cauvet

**300422**
173 × 135 cm
ink on paper
2022
Private collection
Courtesy Ceysson
& Bénétière Gallery
© Cyrille Cauvet

**070222**
172 × 135 cm
ink on paper
2022
Courtesy Ceysson
& Bénétière Gallery
© Cyrille Cauvet

**080123**
174,5 × 137 cm
ink on paper
2023
Private collection
Courtesy Ceysson
& Bénétière Gallery
© Cyrille Cauvet

**131021**
170 × 135 cm
ink on paper
2021
Private collection
© Fabrice Seixas

**060422**
170 × 136 cm
ink on paper
2022
Banque du
Luxembourg
collection
Courtesy Ceysson
& Bénétière Gallery
© Fabrice Seixas

**010921**
161 × 135 cm
ink on paper
2021
Private collection
© Fabrice Seixas

**210621**
173,5 × 136 cm
ink on paper
2021
Musée Paul Dini
Villefranche-
sur-Saône collection
© Fabrice Seixas

**220521**
169,5 × 135,5 cm
ink on paper
2021
Private collection
© Fabrice Seixas

**251220**
42 × 27 cm
colored pencils
on paper
2020
Private collection
Courtesy Ceysson
& Bénétière Gallery
© Fabrice Seixas

**061221**
46,5 × 31,5 cm
colored pencils
on paper
2021
Courtesy Ceysson
& Bénétière Gallery
© Fabrice Seixas

**051221**
46,5 × 31,5 cm
colored pencils
on paper
2021
Courtesy Ceysson
& Bénétière Gallery
© Fabrice Seixas

**230121**
41 × 27 cm
colored pencils
on paper
2021
Private collection
© Fabrice Seixas

**060819**
41,5 × 27 cm
colored pencils
on paper, 2019
Private collection
Courtesy THE PILL®
Gallery
© Fabrice Seixas

**030921**
46,5 × 31,5 cm
colored pencils
on paper
2021
Courtesy Ceysson
& Bénétière Gallery
© Fabrice Seixas

**171121**
46,5 × 31,5 cm
colored pencils
on paper
2021
Private collection
© Fabrice Seixas

**141121**
46,5 × 31,5 cm
colored pencils
on paper
2021
Courtesy THE PILL®
Gallery
© Fabrice Seixas

**011221**
46,5 × 31,5 cm
colored pencils
on paper
2021
Courtesy Ceysson
& Bénétière Gallery
© Fabrice Seixas

**090921**
46,5 × 31,5 cm
colored pencils
on paper
2021
Courtesy Ceysson
& Bénétière Gallery
© Fabrice Seixas

**120519**
156 × 133.5 cm
ink on paper
2019
Private collection
© Fabrice Seixas

**141020**
173 × 134 cm
ink on paper
2020
Private collection
© Fabrice Seixas

**251220**
155,5 × 134 cm
ink on paper
2020
Private collection
© Fabrice Seixas

**070319**
160,5 × 135,5 cm
ink on paper
2019
Courtesy THE PILL®
Gallery
© Fabrice Seixas

**011019**
161 × 134,5 cm
ink on paper
2019
Courtesy THE PILL®
Gallery
© Fabrice Seixas

**130319**
172 × 133 cm
ink on paper
2019
Private collection
Courtesy Ceysson
& Bénétière Gallery
© Fabrice Seixas

**230521**
163,5 × 104,5 cm
ink on paper
2021
Private collection
© Fabrice Seixas

**040420**
161,5 × 132,5 cm
ink on paper
2020
Private collection
Courtesy galerie
Ceysson & Bénétière
© Fabrice Seixas

**240521**
158,5 × 105,5 cm
ink on paper
2021
Private collection
© Fabrice Seixas

**270521**
168 × 112 cm
ink on paper
2021
Private collection
© Fabrice Seixas

**010321**
166 × 135 cm
ink on paper
2021
Private collection
© Fabrice Seixas

**CCLXXXVI**
149,8 × 132,4 cm
ink on paper
2014
Courtesy Ceysson
& Bénétière Gallery

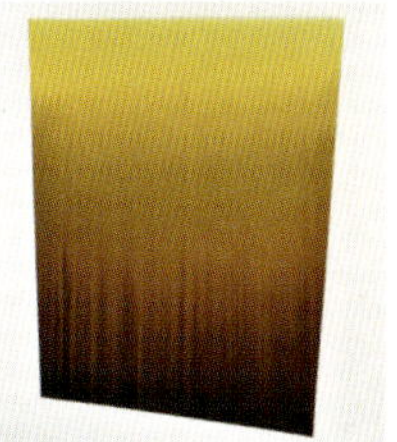

**CCCV**
144 × 133 cm
ink on paper
2015
Courtesy Galerie
THE PILL®
© Rebecca Fanuele

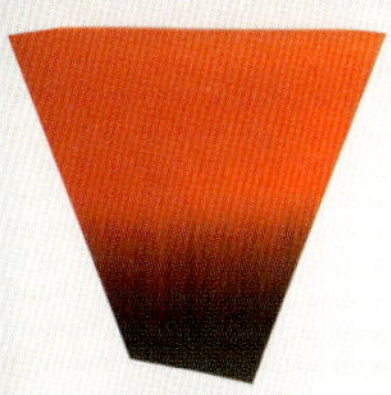

**CCLXXII**
137 × 132 cm
ink on paper
2013
FRAC Auvergne
collection
Clermont-Ferrand
© Ludovic Combe

**CCLXXX**
139 × 133 cm
ink on paper
2013
Private collection

**CCLXXIV**
140 × 134 cm
ink on paper
2013
FRAC Auvergne
collection
Clermont-Ferrand
© Ludovic Combe

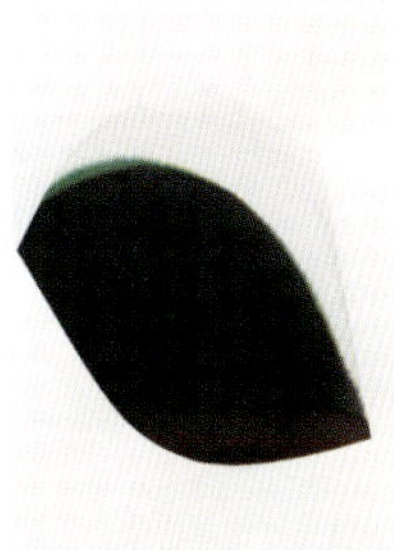

**801.8**
51 × 36 cm
ink on paper
2011
Courtesy THE PILL®
Gallery
© Laura Morsch

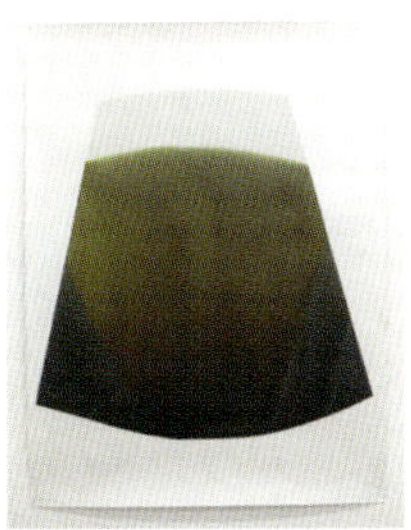

**CLXIV**
150 × 114 cm
ink on paper
2012
Courtesy Galerie
THE PILL®

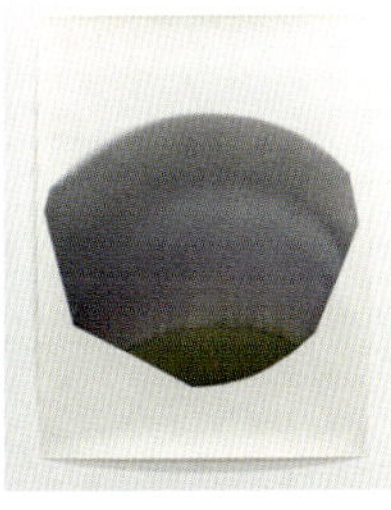

**CLXVI**
150 × 114 cm
ink on paper
2012
Courtesy THE PILL®
Gallery

**XC**
140 × 114 cm
ink on paper
2010
agnès b. collection
© Laura Morsch

**CXVIII**
150 × 114 cm
ink on paper
2011
agnès b. collection
© Laura Morsch

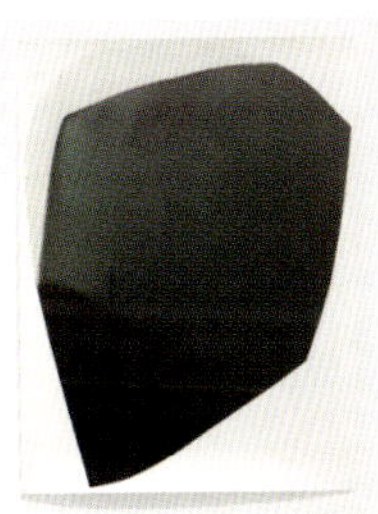

**CXC**
147 × 114 cm
ink on paper
2011
Courtesy THE PILL®
Gallery
© Laura Morsch

**XCVIII**
132 × 114 cm
ink on paper
2010
Courtesy Galerie
THE PILL®
© Laura Morsch

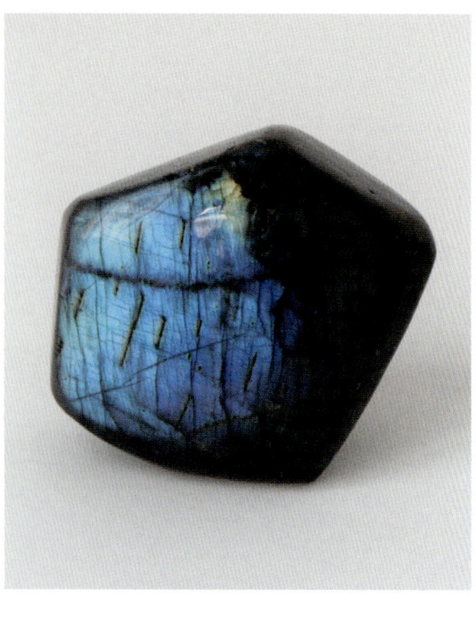

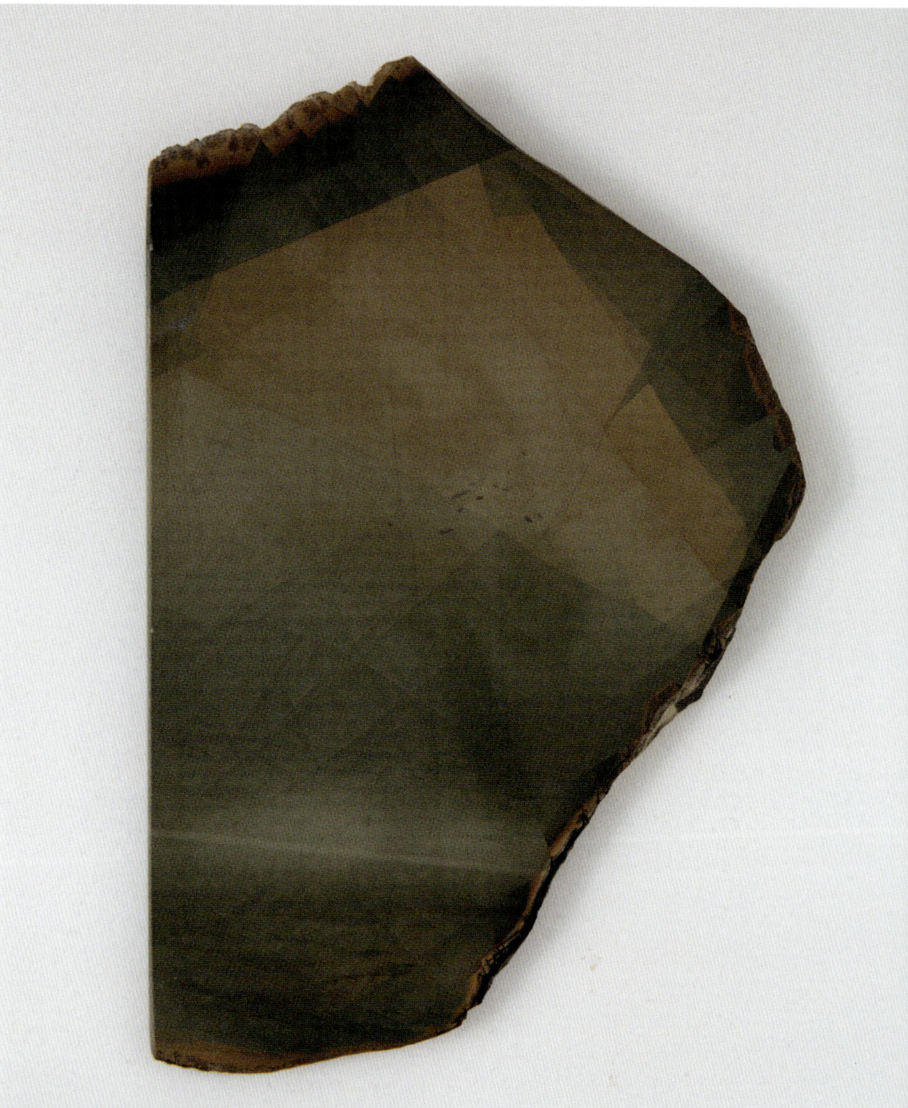

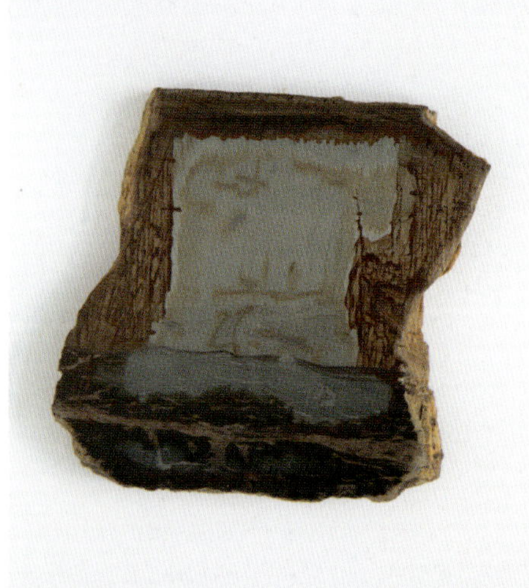

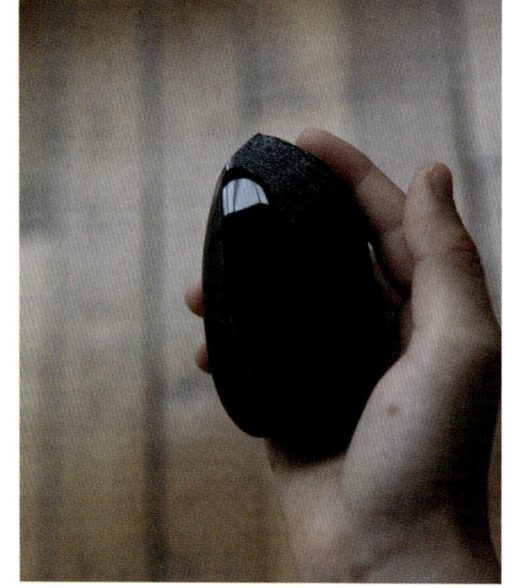

Labradorite, paesines, obsidian collected by the artist

Claire Chesnier (b. 1986) first encountered art through music and writing, which she practiced from an early age. She devoted almost twenty years to classical and contemporary dance. Painting, which she has been practicing since the beginning, is "the decisive encounter experienced as an extension of the writing gesture and the embodiment of an expanded dance gesture". Her commitment to painting is turned towards a physical and poetic relationship with the world, the apprehension of touch, the sensitive embrace of things, of life. As she puts it, "painting is about touch, about how to touch and be touched. It reaches where words fail, through tactility and rhythm".

"Her paintings achieve a power of elevation towards the atmospheric, in their visible abstraction, their pigment charge and their material liquidity. Their verticality, based on the proportions of the body, paradoxically swings towards the horizontality of a tremolo, a stripe of chromatic gradations that runs right through the paintings. Two axes are superimposed, that of the body and that of an expanse of landscape, making it impossible to reconstitute the painting's stages. They are dawns over abstraction, ajours of light whose spectrum unfolds in elusive ranges. Faced with these colors arranged like a reflection of water, a chalky dermis, a metallic moiré, the viewer is left to dwell in the most literal sense of the word. The surface is the home of the gaze, invited to soak up what, after the deliquescent sludge of the creative process, after the drying out of the mixing colors, reveals itself to the viewer in a succession of subtle chromatic apparitions, pictorial phosphenes, slow upheavals accompanied by the fluctuations of daylight. An abstraction perhaps, but one that neither detaches nor disengages us from reality or sensation. To look at Claire Chesnier's paintings is to ride the wings of length and light in the vice of passing time and embodied painting, restoring meaning to the notion of the gaze: revelation of the perceptible sensitive world, ceaselessly reiterated focus, dazzlement, lucidity, sequences of clairvoyance, withdrawal, loss, *recovery*—as one *recovers* sight after temporary blindness." (Jean-Charles Vergne)

Claire Chesnier is a graduate of the École Nationale Supérieure des Beaux-Arts de Paris and the Université Paris 1 Panthéon-Sorbonne, where she obtained a doctorate in Art and Art Sciences. She was quickly noticed by fashion designer agnès b., who awarded her the Prix des Amis des Beaux-Arts in 2011 and brought her into her gallery, Galerie du jour agnès b., where they collaborated from 2012 to 2017. This was followed by a collaboration with Galerie ETC in Paris from 2018 to 2022. She is now represented by Ceysson & Bénétière (Paris, New York, Tokyo, Luxembourg, Saint-Etienne, Lyon, Geneva) and THE PILL® (Paris, Istanbul). She lives and works in Paris.

She has won several awards, including the Prix des Amis des Beaux-Arts, the Prix des Talents Contemporains from the Fondation François Schneider, the Prix Art Collector, the Prix Fénéon from the Chancellerie des Universités de Paris and the Prix Yishu 8 from the House of Arts of Beijing.

In 2025, the CCC-OD (Tours) presents a solo show entitled *Une éclaircie à la verticale*, a broad overview of her career. The same year, she was invited by the Musée de l'Orangerie to take part in the exhibition *Dans le Flou*, where she exhibited alongside Mark Rothko, Hans Hartung, Gerhard Richter, Claude Monet and William Turner, among others. The exhibition then travels to the CaixaForum in Madrid and Barcelona.

## PERSONAL EXHIBITIONS (selection)

2025 *Une éclaircie à la verticale*, cur. Isabelle Reiher, Marine Rochard, CCC-OD, Tours, FR
*Claire Chesnier*, THE PILL® Gallery, Istanbul, TR

2024 *Un rose, une rosée, un couchant*, text by Maylis de Kerangal, Ceysson & Bénétière Gallery, Paris, FR

2023 *Rayer le jour, le soir étain,* text by Itzhak Goldberg, Ceysson & Bénétière Gallery, Lyon, FR
*Les Jours*, cur. Philippe Piguet, Chapelle de la Visitation, Centre d'Art de Thonon-les-Bains, FR

2022 *Mudhoney, Claire Chesnier - Denis Laget*, cur. Jean-Charles Vergne, ETC Gallery, Paris, FR

2021 *Par espacements et par apparitions,* text by Pierre Wat, l'ahah, Paris, FR

2020 *Le ciel aussi est un fracas*, cur. Karim Ghaddab, ETC Gallery, Paris, FR

2019 *L'Art dans les chapelles*, cur. Éric Suchère, Chapelle de la Trinité Castennec, Bieuzy, FR
*Une réserve de nuit, Claire Chesnier - Estèla Alliaud*, cur. John Cornu, Art & Essai Gallery, Rennes, FR

2018 *Under B shall come Butterfly powder*, Maior Gallery, Palma de Majorque, ES
*Fragments d'une déposition*, Espace Commines, Paris, FR

2016 *Résonances*, Galerie du jour agnès b., Paris, FR

2014 *L'aire des aurores*, cur. Léa Bismuth, le Patio, Paris, FR

2013 *Résonance*, Yishu 8 Maison des Arts, Pékin, CN

2012 *Fragments d'une déposition*, Galerie du jour agnès b., Paris, FR
*Fragments d'une déposition*, agnès b. Gallery, Marseille, FR
*Parcours Saint-Germain*, agnès b., Paris, FR
*Re-veiling*, T-Gallery, Bratislava, SVK


## COLLECTIVE EXHIBITIONS (selection)

2025 *Dans le flou, des années 1950 à nos jours*, cur. Claire Bernardi, Emilia Philippot, Musée de l'Orangerie, Paris, FR, CaixaForum, Madrid, ES, CaixaForum, Barcelone, ES
*Format paysage*, cur. Anne Favier, Ceysson & Bénétière Gallery, Lyon, FR
*Collective*, THE PILL® Gallery, Paris, FR

2024 *Le Jour des peintres*, cur. Nicolas Gausserand, Thomas Lévy-Lasne, Musée d'Orsay, Paris, FR
*Monomania*, Michael Woolworth Publications, Paris, FR
*The Colour Out of Space*, cur. Jean-Charles Vergne, THE PILL®, Istanbul, TR
*Tokyo Gendaï Art Fair*, THE PILL® Gallery, Tokyo, JP
*Collective,* Ceysson & Bénétière Gallery, Paris, FR
*Histoire d'Yishu 8,* National Art Museum of China, Pékin, CN
*Les Lois de L'imaginaire*, cur. Laure Forlay, FRAC Auvergne, Musées d'Aurillac, FR

2023 *Le Toucher du monde*, cur. Sylvie Carlier, Laure Forlay, Jean-Charles Vergne, Musée Paul Dini, Villefranche-sur-Saône, FR
*Beautés*, cur. Jean-Charles Vergne, FRAC Auvergne, Clermont-Ferrand, FR
*Perceptions*, cur. Élodie Derval, Musées d'Angers-Artothèque, Angers, FR
*Mirages*, cur. Nicolas Dhervillers, Claire Gastaud Gallery, Clermont-Ferrand, FR

2022 *À contre-jour, dialogue avec Eugène Leroy*, cur. Germain Hirselj, Mélanie Lerrat, Christelle Manfredi, Musée des Beaux-Arts Eugène Leroy MUba, Tourcoing, FR
*Yishu 8, Dialogue avec les Collections du Musée Guimet*, cur. Sophie Makariou, Henry-Claude Cousseau, Musée Guimet, Paris, FR
*Le Promontoire du songe*, cur. Jean-Charles Vergne, FRAC Auvergne, Clermont-Ferrand, FR

2021 *Printtemps*, Fondation Fiminco, Romainville, FR
*Inspiré.e.s*, cur. Lucile Hitier, Centre d'art l'ArTsenal, Dreux, FR
*April Showers Bring May Flowers*, Michael Woolworth Publications, Paris, FR

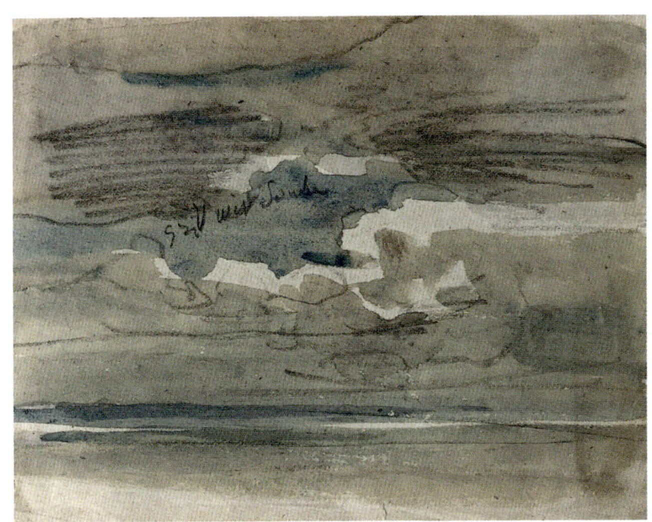

Eugène Boudin, *Étude de ciel sur la mer*, circa 1865-1870, watercolor, graphite on paper, 14 x 18,50 cm, private collection

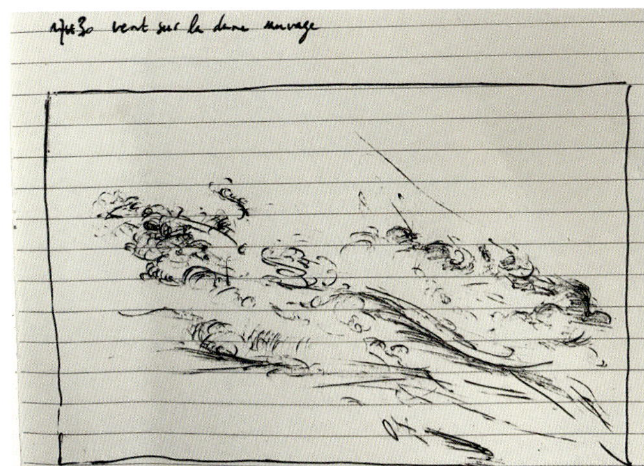

Claire Chesnier, notebook, 2024, *17h30 wind on the wild dune*

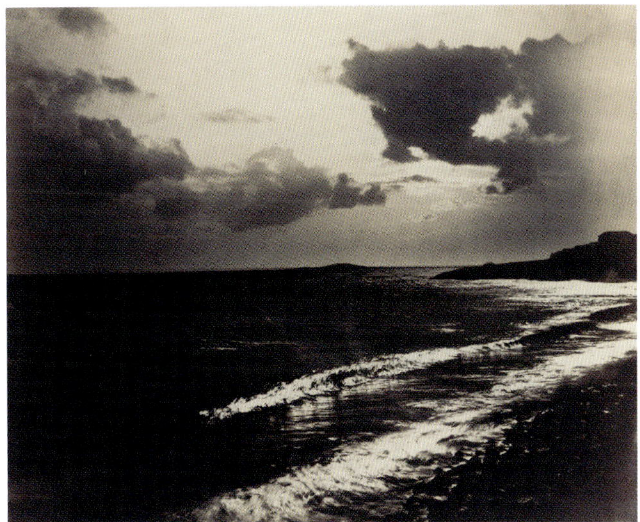

Gustave Le Gray, *Grande Lame, Méditerranée, N°19*, albumen print from two collodion glass negatives, Bibliothèque nationale de France, 1857

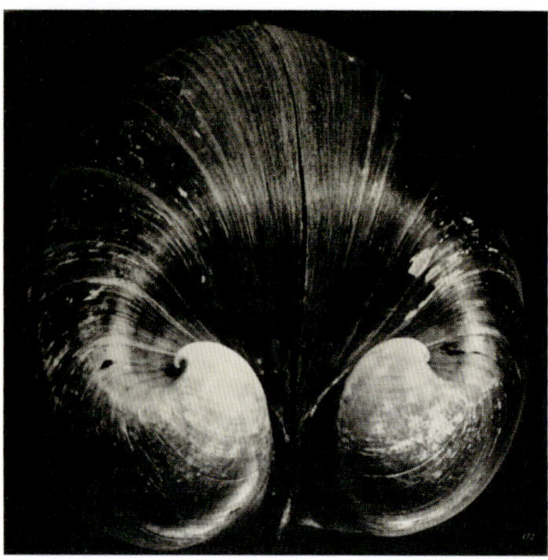

Shell Glossus humanus

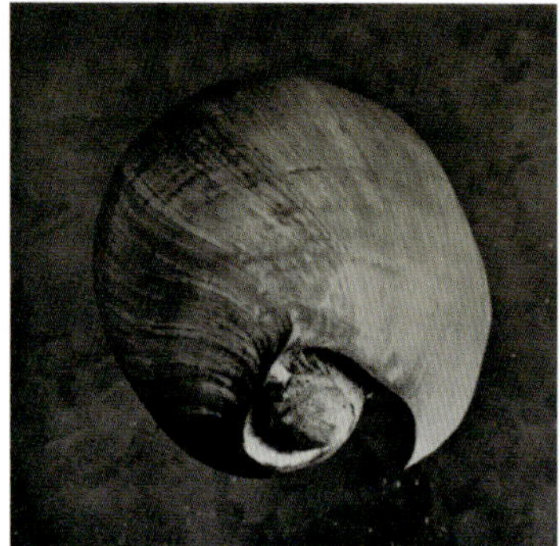

Shell Cymbium cymbium

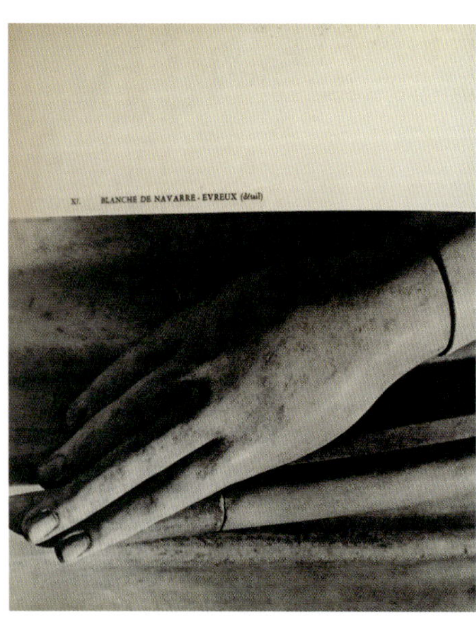

Tomb of Blanche de Navarre-Evreux (detail), Basilique de Saint-Denis, second half of 14<sup>th</sup> century

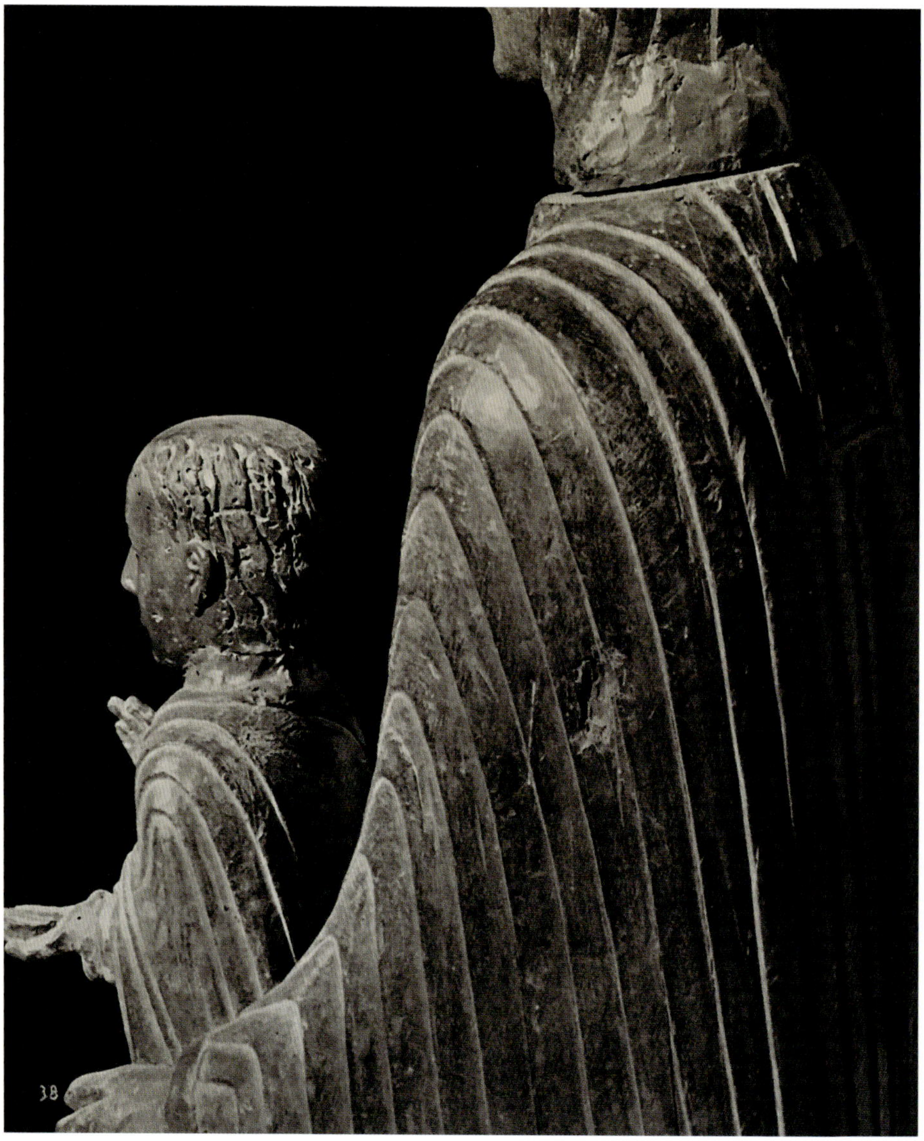

Romanesque Virgin in Majesty, Notre-Dame de Vauclair, Molompize, 12<sup>th</sup> century

*Collection Gilles Balmet*, cur. Gilles Balmet, Pavillon Carré de Baudouin, Paris, FR
*Les Apparences*, cur. Thomas Lévy-Lasne, Centre d'Art À cent mètres du centre du monde, Perpignan, FR

2020    *Hors champ et paysages, Collection agnès b.*, cur. Jean de Loisy, La Fab' agnès b., Paris, FR
*The Painting people*, Michael Woolworth Publications, Paris, FR

2019    *Some of Us, an Overview of French Art Scene*, NordArt, cur. Jérôme Cotinet-Alphaize, Marianne Derrien, Kunstwerk Carlshütte, Budelsdorf, DE
*Résurgence III: Dimension supplémentaire*, cur. Valentine Boé, Artothèque du Lot, Souillac, FR

2018    *Vertiges, une chute dans le vide du ciel*, cur. Léa Bismuth, LaBanque, Béthune, FR
*Secrets d'ateliers*, Jean-Paul Barrès Gallery, Toulouse, FR
*Eclectic*, Maior Gallery, Pollença, Majorque, ES
*Fading away*, cur. Céline Flécheux, Rosario Caltabiano, 22,48m$^2$ Gallery, Paris, FR

2017    *Aurores*, Pauline Pavec Gallery, Paris, FR
*Cinq fois deux*, cur. Philippe Piguet, la Patinoire Royale, Bruxelles, BE
*Vantablack*, cur. Erik Verhagen et Jocelyn Wolff, Jocelyn Wolff Gallery, Paris, FR
*Peindre dit-elle chap. 2*, cur. Julie Crenn, Annabelle Ténèze, Amélie Lavin, Musée des Beaux-Arts de Dole, FR

2016    *À quoi tient la beauté des étreintes*, cur. Jean-Charles Vergne, FRAC Auvergne, Clermont-Ferrand, FR
*Histoire des formes*, cur. Éric Degoutte, Centre d'art Les Tanneries, Amilly, FR
*Cinq fois deux*, cur. Philippe Piguet, le Patio, Paris, FR
*Virage*, Galerie de Roussan, Paris, FR
*Peindre n'est(-ce) pas teindre?*, cur. Sandrine Morsillo, Musée de la toile de Jouy, Jouy-en-Josas, FR

2015    *Minéral*, cur. Jean-Marie Gallais and Ludovic Delalande, Max Hetzler Gallery, Paris, FR
*Un regard sur la collection agnès b.*, cur. Marc Donnadieu, Lille métropole musée d'art moderne, d'art contemporain et d'art brut (LaM), Villeneuve d'Ascq, FR
*Traits d'esprit*, Galerie du jour agnès b., Paris, FR
*Ouvrages de dames*, cur. Dominique Païni, Valérie Delaunay Gallery, Paris, FR

2014    *Avec et sans peinture*, Musée d'Art Contemporain du Val-de-Marne (MAC VAL), Vitry-sur-Seine, FR
*Et la peinture...?*, Galerie du jour agnès b., Paris, FR
*Talents Contemporains*, François Schneider Foundation, Fondation de France, Wattwiller, FR
*Biennale du dessin*, cur. Emmanuelle Brugerolles, Gilgian Gelzer, Bernard Moninot, Cité Internationale des Arts, Paris, FR

2013    *The Drawer*, Ed. The Drawer, Galerie du jour agnès b., Paris, FR
*Bruissements* (*Nouvelles vagues,* Palais de Tokyo), cur. Léa Bismuth, Isabelle Gounod Gallery, Paris, FR
*Sur la mauvaise pente* (*Nouvelles vagues*, Palais de Tokyo), cur. Nabila Mokrani, Galerie de Roussan, Paris, FR
*Art Osaka*, Jeune Création, Japan French Institute-Kansai, Hotel Granvia, Osaka, JP
*Ce que le sonore fait au visuel*, Château de Servières, Marseille, FR
*Last dance*, cur. Le Syndicat Magnifique, Galerie Gourvennec Ogor, Marseille, FR
*La rime et la raison*, cur. MPVITE, Label hypothèse, l'Escaut, Bruxelles, BE
*Fondation*, Leonardo Agosti Gallery, Sète, FR
*La dispute de l'âme et du corps*, cur. Jean-Christophe Arcos, Cloître des Billettes, Paris, FR
*Emergence*, cur. Katrin Bremermann, Yifat Gat, Erin Lawlor, Hotel Sauroy, Paris, FR

2012    *Filiations - Dialogues avec les œuvres de la Donation Albers-Honegger*, cur. Fabienne Fulchéri, Alexandra Deslys, Espace de l'Art Concret, Château de Mouans-Sartoux, FR
*Jeune Création*, le Centquatre, Paris, FR

| | |
|---|---|
| | *Décalage*, Espace Commines, Paris, FR |
| | *Ready for Fatality?*, Fabienne Bideaud, Berlin French Institute, Note on, Berlin, DE |
| | *Blank Generation, Salon de Montrouge*, le Beffroi, Montrouge, FR |
| | *Biennale de la Jeune Création*, La Graineterie, Houilles, FR |
| | *Figures du sommeil*, cur. Catherine Viollet, Jean Collet Gallery, Vitry-sur-Seine, FR |
| 2011 | *Comme elle vient*, cur. Label hypothèse, Rosenblum Collection & Friends, Paris, FR |
| | *Prix des Amis des Beaux-Arts de Paris*, ENSBA, Paris, FR |
| | *Prix International de Peinture J.-M. Mourlot* (Fondation de France), Jeu de Paume Gallery, Marseille, FR |
| 2010 | *Prix International de Peinture*, Jean Collet Gallery, Vitry-sur-Seine, FR |
| 2009 | *Kiitos II*, Musée des Arts et Métiers, Paris, FR |

## COLLECTIONS (selection)

FRAC Auvergne Collection, Clermont-Ferrand, FR
Musée Paul Dini Collection, Villefranche-sur-Saône
agnès b. Collection - La Fab', Paris
Fondation François Schneider Collection, Fondation de France, Wattwiller
Ville de Vitry-sur-Seine Collection, on deposit at the Musée d'Art Contemporain du Val-de-Marne (MAC VAL)
Banque du Luxembourg Collection
Musées d'Angers Collection - Artothèque, Angers
Artothèque du Lot Collection
Yishu 8 House of the Arts of Beijing Collection
Art Collector Collection, Paris

## PUBLICATIONS (selection)

| | |
|---|---|
| 2024 | *Sam Francis*, dir. Pierre Wat, "La limite du ciel", text by Claire Chesnier, Coll. Transatlantique, ER Publishing, Paris |
| | *Some of Us*, dir. Marianne Derrien, Jérôme Cotinet-Alphaize, Ed. Manuella, Paris |
| | *Fragments*, dir. Camille Saint-Jacques, Éric Suchère, "Brisées", text by Claire Chesnier, Coll. Beautés, Ed. L'Atelier contemporain, Strasbourg |
| 2023 | *Claire Chesnier - Les Jours, Semaine* 03.23, dir. Philippe Piguet, Chapelle de la Visitation, Thonon-les-Bains |
| | *Beautés*, Jean-Charles Vergne, FRAC Auvergne, Clermont-Ferrand |
| | *Art & Essai, 2014-2020*, dir. John Cornu, Ed. Art & Essai - Université Rennes 2 & cultureclub-studio, Rennes |
| | *Beautés*, dir. Camille Saint-Jacques, Éric Suchère, "Beautés", text by Claire Chesnier, Coll. Beautés, Ed. L'Atelier contemporain & FRAC Auvergne, Strasbourg |
| | *L'horizon d'un instant*, Pierre Cendors, Claire Chesnier, Ed. L'Atelier contemporain, Strasbourg |
| 2022 | *Le Promontoire du songe*, Jean-Charles Vergne, FRAC Auvergne, Clermont-Ferrand |
| 2021 | *Mudhoney*, Claire Chesnier - Denis Laget, Jean-Charles Vergne, ETC Gallery, Paris |
| 2020 | *Le ciel aussi est un fracas*, Claire Chesnier, Karim Ghaddab, ETC Gallery, Paris |
| | *L'Art dans les chapelles*, dir. Éric Suchère, L'Art dans les chapelles, Pontivy |
| | *La Besogne des images*, dir. Léa Bismuth, Mathilde Girard, Ed. Filigranes, Paris |
| 2018 | *Un lieu, loin, ici*, Antoine Émaz, Claire Chesnier, dir. Armand Dupuy, Jeremy Liron, Coll. Livres d'artistes, Ed. Centrifuges, Saint-Jean La Buissière |
| | *Peindre dit-elle - chapitre 2*, dir. Julie Crenn, Annabelle Ténèze, Amélie Lavin, Musée des Beaux Arts de Dole |
| 2014 | *Claire Chesnier - L'aire des aurores*, dir. Léa Bismuth, Art Collector, Paris |
| | *Avec et sans peinture*, Ed. Musée d'Art Contemporain du Val-de-Marne (MAC VAL), Vitry-sur-Seine |

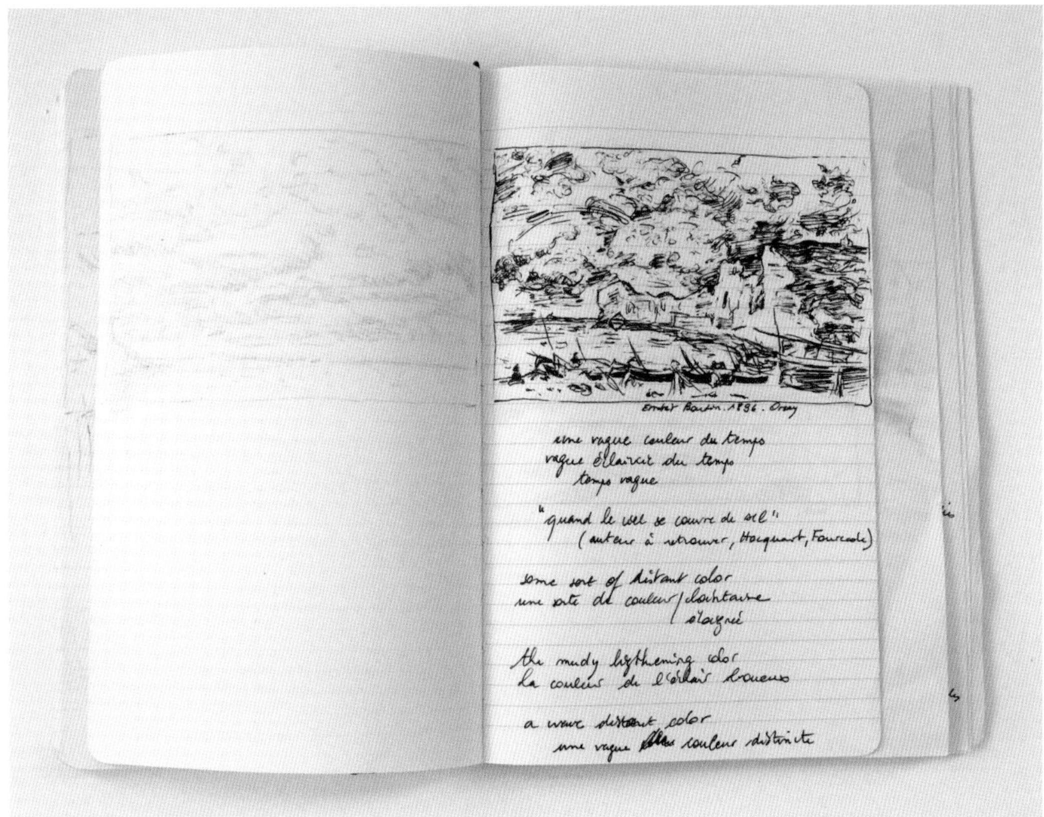


Claire Chesnier, notebook

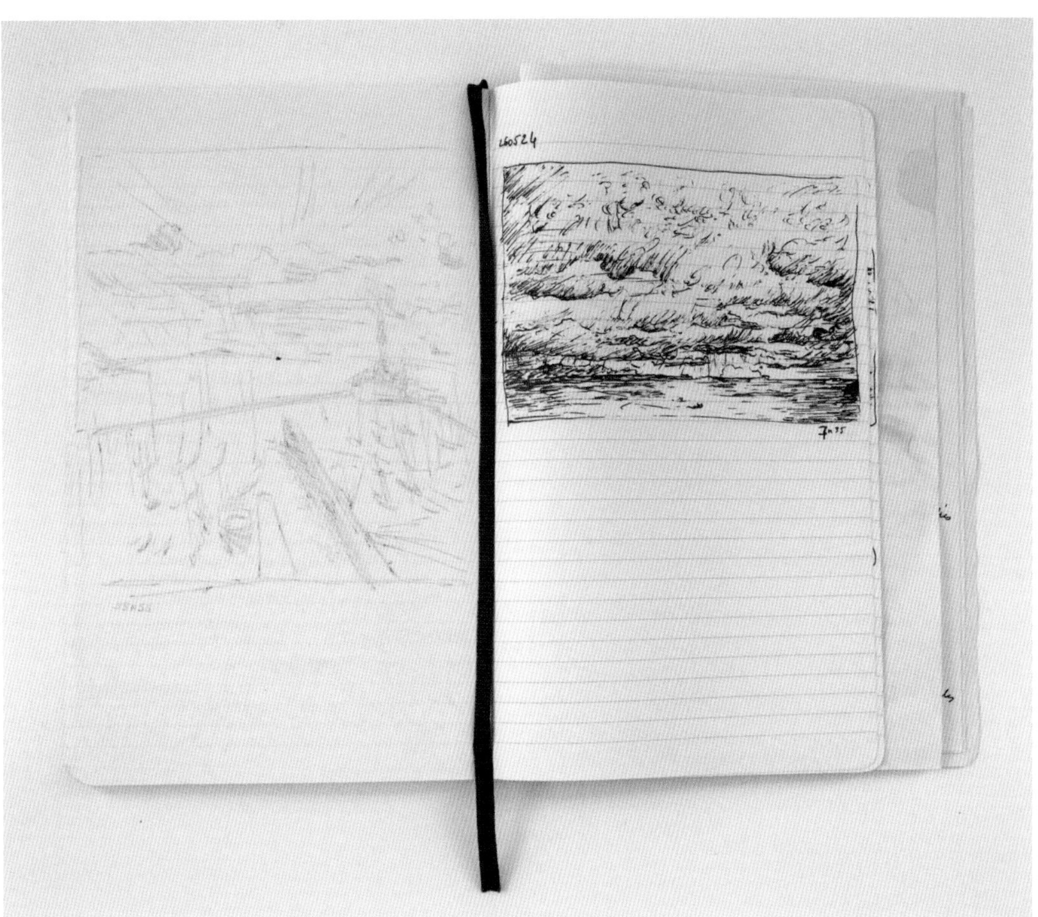


Claire Chesnier, notebook

**MAYLIS
DE KERANGAL**

Maylis de Kerangal is the author of over fifteen novels and short stories, translated into many languages. They include *Corniche Kennedy* (2008), *Naissance d'un pont* (2010), fiction about a major construction site in an imaginary city, and *Tangente vers l'Est* (2012), fiction about a trip on the Trans-Siberian Railway. In 2014, *Réparer les vivants*, a novel about a heart transplant, won a dozen literary prizes and was adapted for film and theater. Published the same year, *À ce stade de la nuit*, a nocturne about shipwrecks in the Mediterranean, won the Prix Boccace in 2016. In 2018, she published *Un monde à portée de main*, an introductory novel to painting that questions creation. In May 2021, she publishes *Canoës*, dedicated to the exploration of the human voice. Her work questions the landscape and the imprint of places. Her writing is characterized by attention to detail, the use of documents and investigation. Her latest novel, *Jour de ressac*, was published in 2024.

**MOLLY WARNOCK**

Molly Warnock is a historian and critic of the visual arts primarily in Europe and the United States from early 20th-century modernism to the present. The author of the monographs, *Simon Hantaï and the Reserves of Painting* (Pennsylvania State University Press, 2020) and *Penser la Peinture: Simon Hantaï* (Gallimard, 2012), she has written widely on modern and contemporary art for, among other journals, *Artforum, Art in America, Les Cahiers du Musée National d'Art Moderne*, *Tate Papers*, and *Journal of Contemporary Painting*, as well as for numerous exhibition catalogs. She has also edited four volumes for the *Transatlantique* collection (ER Publishing), on Martin Barré, Simon Hantaï, James Bishop, and Michel Parmentier. Currently, she is Director of the Clyfford Still Catalogue Raisonné Project at the Clyfford Still Museum in Denver, Colorado.

**PIERRE WAT**

Pierre Wat is Professor of Art History at Panthéon-Sorbonne University, Paris I. A specialist in European Romanticism, he has published *Naissance de l'art romantique* (Flammarion 1998, reissued coll. Champs Arts 2013), *Constable* (Hazan, 2002) and *Turner, menteur magnifique* (Hazan, 2010). He is also the author of studies on contemporary art: *Pierre Buraglio*, (Flammarion, 2001), *Claude Viallat* (Hazan, 2006), *Frédéric Benrath* (Hazan, 2016). Latest publications: *Pérégrinations. Paysages entre nature et histoire* (Hazan, 2017), and *Hans Hartung, la peinture pour mémoire* (Hazan, 2019). In 2023-2024, he was guest curator of the Nicolas de Staël retrospective at the Musée d'Art Moderne in Paris, and at the Fondation de l'Hermitage in Lausanne. In 2025, at the Kunsthalle Praha (Prague), he is preparing the first joint exhibition of works by Anna-Eva Bergman and Hans Hartung.

**JEAN-MICHEL
ALBEROLA**

Born in Saïda, Algeria, in 1953, Jean-Michel Alberola lives and works in Paris. For the past thirty years, he has been producing a multi-faceted body of work ranging from figurative to abstract and conceptual art. Gouaches, neon lights, sculptures, artists' books and films are the various facets of a body of work that questions the fragility of beauty, the ambiguity of the gaze, the role of the artist and the purpose of art. With humor and poetry, this committed artist combines artistic reflection with political and social questioning. In 1985, the Centre Pompidou held a solo exhibition of his work entitled "La Peinture, l'Histoire et la Géographie" (Painting, History and Geography). He has had numerous exhibitions in major museums such as the Musée d'art Moderne in Paris and the Palais de Tokyo. A long-time professor at the École Nationale Supérieure des Beaux-Arts de Paris, he is now one of France's leading artistic personalities. He was Claire Chesnier's studio manager from 2008 to 2011.

Claire Chesnier warmly thanks all those who contributed to this book for their precious help, their trust and their attentive eye:

**THE PILL® Gallery, Paris/Istanbul**
Suela Cennet, Jean-Charles Vergne, Alca Agabeyoglu, Asli Seven

**Ceysson & Bénétière Gallery, Paris/New York/Tokyo/ Saint-Etienne/Lyon/ Luxembourg/Genève/Panéry**
Loïc Bénétière, Loïc Garrier, Bernard Ceysson, François Ceysson, Maëlle Ebelle, Pierre Collet, Leslie You, Ivana Garel, Clémence Boisanté, Jonquille Pfister, Marie Estienne

**L'ahah, Paris**
**Endowment Fund Pascaline Mulliez**
Pascaline Mulliez, Olivier Delavallade, Doria Tichit

**The CCC OD, Centre de Création Contemporaine Olivier Debré, Tours**
Isabelle Reiher, Marine Rochard

**ADAGP**

**JBE BOOKS**
David Desrimais, Emma Zampieri, Lisa Valentin

**Olumee**
Arnaud Lejeune, Guillaume Lejeune, Jean-Yves Moulin

**Authors**
Maylis de Kerangal, Molly Warnock, Pierre Wat, Jean-Michel Alberola

**Translators**
Laurie Hurwitz, Mériam Korichi

**as well as:**
Alexandra Alquier, Rémy Bardin, Thomas Benhamou, Sereine Berlottier, Claire Bernardi, Claire et Philippe Bettinelli, Léa Bismuth, Alain Bonfand, Marianne Bouctot, Laure Bouery, Jean-Pierre Bretheau, Marie Cantos, Sylvie Carlier, Christine Cayol, Josette et Jacques Chesnier, Ivan Chesnier, Michael Chesnier, Sylvie Chesnier, Bertille Cougul, Arnaud Courtois, Henri-Claude Cousseau, Juliette Degennes, Charlotte Denoël, Evelyne et Jacques Deret, Marianne Derrien, Marc Desgrandchamps, François-Marie Deyrolle, Vincent Dulom, Sylvie Dupuy, Sarah El Idrissi, Antoine Émaz, Marie-Christine et Laurent Etellin, Jean-Charles Eustache, Jacques Font, Karim Ghaddab, Marie-Christine et Bernard Guibert, Olivier Harlingue, Martine et Marc Jardinier, Nathalie Koble, Elizabeth Landers, Arnaud Laporte, Isabelle Lartault, Thomas Lévy-Lasne, Isabelle Marchesin, Alexandra Maurice, Agnès Mentre, Eva Nielsen, Marine Normand, Lou-Gabriel Paris, Emilia Philippot, Isabelle Pigé, Philippe Piguet, Christophe Pillet, Marguerite Pilven, Nathalie Ratinier, Didier Renault, Ariane Requin, Corinne Rondeau, Sébastien Rongier, Charlotte Rouget, Fabrice Seixas, Pierre Sendors, Zrinka Stahuljak, Barbara Stehle, Éric Suchère, François Trausch, Agnès Troublé (agnès b.), Éric Verhagen, Michel Verjux, Prune Vidal, Michael Woolworth, Véronique Yersin

and those who wished to remain anonymous.

**Editorial direction**
David Desrimais and Jean-Charles Vergne

**Editorial coordination**
Lisa Valentin

**Iconographic support**
Fabrice Seixas

**Graphic design**
Emma Zampieri – Studio JBE

**Proofreading**
Cassandra Katsiaficas
Sarah El Idrissi

**Translation**
Laurie Hurvitz

**Photoengraving**
IGS-Print

**Typefaces**
Helvetica Neue
Castoro

With the support of ADAGP,
Bourse collection Monographie 2024

With the participation of Ceysson & Bénétière Gallery, L'ahah, the Pascaline Mulliez
Endowment Fund and the Centre de création contemporaine Olivier Debré
– CCC OD, Tours (FR) on the occasion of Claire Chesnier's solo exhibition
(galerie blanche) from June 6, 2025 to January 18, 2026.

This publication is part of a collection of books and artist monographs
published in collaboration with THE PILL®.

Printed in Lithuania
Legal deposit: December 2024

JBE Books
90 rue de la Folie-Méricourt
75011 Paris
jbe-books.com

ISBN 978-2-36568-104-9

nuageuse 11
moyen format
ciel tourbe trouble vert
lisière orage rose, même bleue, sol fumé vert
ancien or fumerolles roses

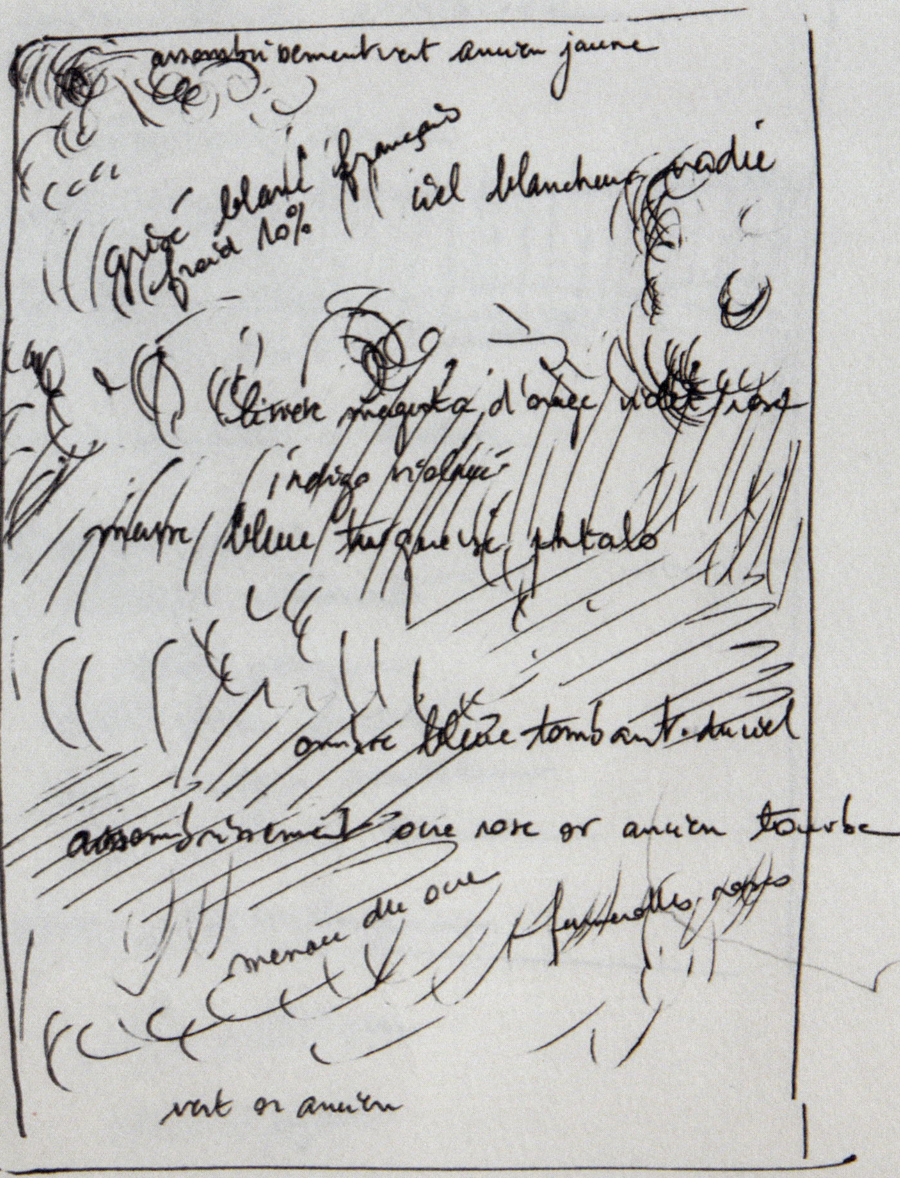

122 × 36,5 cm
encres / papier

* chevron jaune d'or orangé vert
matière pluie brumeuse

gris orageux

bleu gris lourd

légère pluie d'orage

traînées grises / blanc rosé

bleu blanc rosé pluvieux

lumière à la lisière du jaune

veiné jaune d'or chaud
or chaud cuit
jaune orangé vril or

orangé ocre sienne

vert bleu phtalo
vert turquoise
poudre blanchâtre brumeuse
bleu turquoise pluie de front

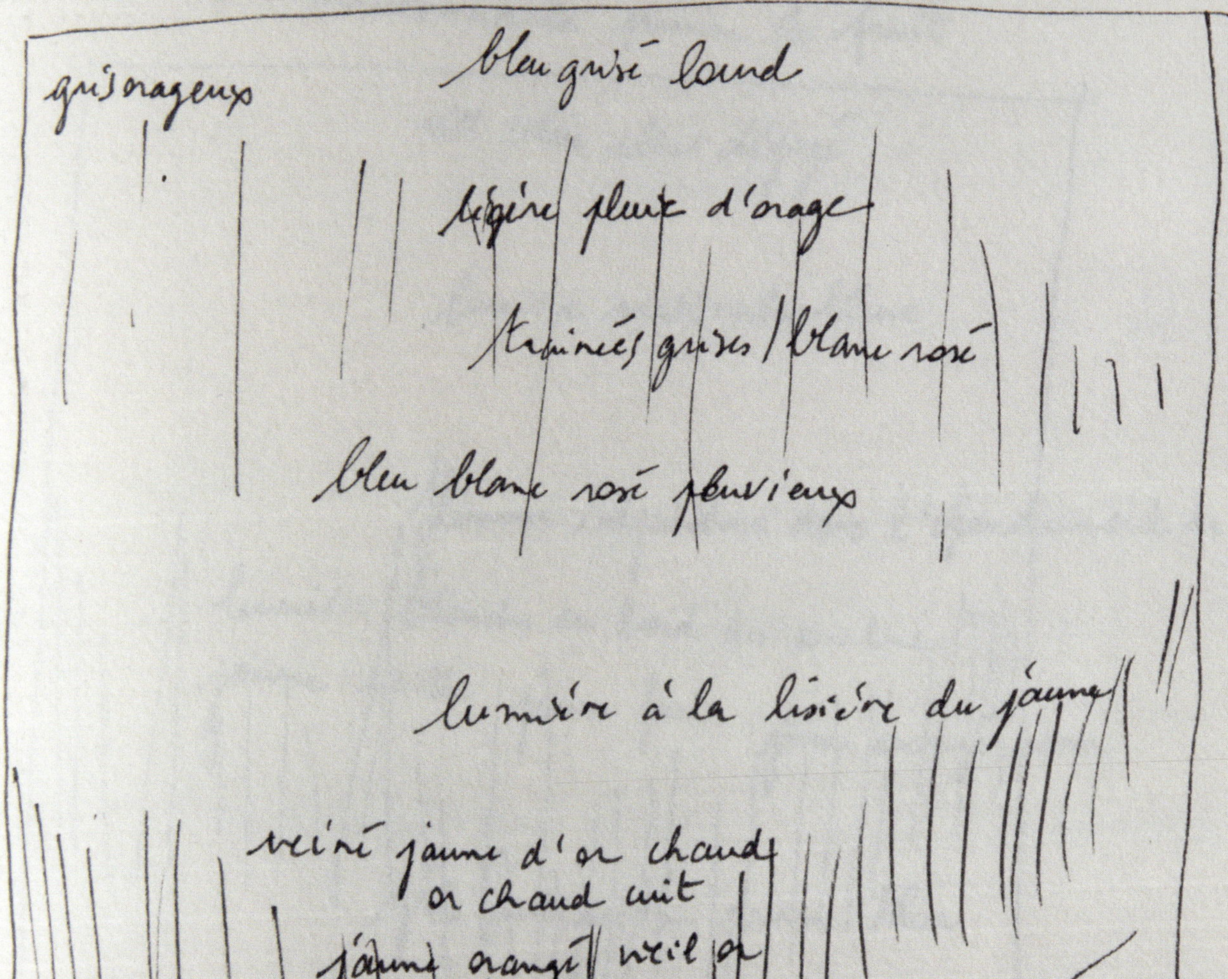

165 x 136 cm

encre s/ papier Fab.